"*Playing Hurt* helped me remember that during my baseball career I played hurt and in pain many timerize was worth the pain, so I didn't giare times in my marriage when my feeliacy is to run to the bench and take a seght I deserved. *Playing Hurt* has helpeuse my wife, marriage, and family are more important than any game I ever pitched or golf tournament I have ever played."

—**Jose Alvarez**, Retired Major League pitcher for the Atlanta Braves, professional golfer, and chaplain to PGA's Nationwide Tour

"I've played nine years in the NFL, won two Super Bowl Championship rings, and had five surgeries—injuries are inevitable in the game. You can't help your team when you're on the bench. The same is true in marriage. Brian coaches you on how to get back in the game and start winning again."

—**Ken Walter**, NFL punter for the Carolina Panthers, Seattle Seahawks, and New England Patriots

"*Playing Hurt* is a book all men will benefit from if they will rise to the challenge to read it. As men, we can either run into passivity, or we can play hurt and enjoy the blessing of a fulfilling marriage and life."

—**Doug Hudson**, founder and president of *The Hub*, www.gotothehub.com

"If married men are looking for encouragement in dealing with the real issues of marriage—[in a book] that is written in a way they can relate to and understand and in a way that applies biblical standards—then they will find it in *Playing Hurt*. Brian Goins does a great job of combining insight and reality, especially in a man's world."

—**Tom Nelson**, pastor of Denton Bible Church and author of *The Book of Romance*

PLAYING HURT

A Guy's Strategy for a Winning Marriage

Brian Goins

Kregel
Publications

Contents

Foreword

I LOVE SPORTS OF ALL KINDS. Baseball, basketball, football, track—you name it. I inherited it from my dad.

My dad's nickname was "Hook" Rainey, not because he was a Captain Hook look-alike, but because he had a wicked curve ball that would blaze its way to the plate and "fall off the table." He played in the St. Louis Cardinals farm system, and in his prime his crooked curve opened the door for him to pitch a game against legendary Hall of Fame pitcher Dizzy Dean.

Hook was a tall lefty who could have made it to the big leagues, but he never had a coach who really trained him. As a result, he played hurt and permanently injured his arm. Who knows what this talented country pitcher could have done with the right coach?

Truly great coaches, ones who are wise, are scarce.

Life coaches, those who know the "game" and are skilled in truly training another man in life skills, are harder to find than box seats to Game 7 at the World Series. And six decades of living have taught me that every man needs life coaching. He needs training in three relationships that he's not naturally good at—his relationships with God, with his spouse, and with his children. Without such a coach, a man is simply not going to take his life and his most important relationships to the level they were designed to be played.

Gentlemen, may I introduce you to your life coach, Brian Goins.

Foreword

I first met Coach Goins when he and his wife joined a team of over 130 elite communicators who are committed to training the next generation of marriages and families through FamilyLife's Weekend to Remember marriage getaways. It didn't take long to understand why Coach Goins is so effective in helping men succeed in their marriages. His passion to come alongside men and equip them is contagious.

He speaks a man's language, and he knows how to move a man's heart. He is one of those rare leaders who not only understands men, but also has a game plan to develop them.

Men respond and play up to their potential when they rub shoulders with Coach Goins. He isn't a critical, verbally abusive teacher; instead, his winsome style motivates them to get into the game with God and with their wives. His "chalk talks" aren't warmed up leftovers from the Casey Stengel era. His fresh, edgy style is more like ESPN Sports Center, making you move forward on the edge of your seat to hear what he has to say next.

He may get in your face, give you a chest butt, and call you to man up. In the end, you know he's right and all the pain will definitely be worth it.

Brian is a no-baloney man. He doesn't sanitize the stories about his marriage. As you read his book, you'll not only be able to relate to him as an imperfect husband, but you will also benefit from his transparency and the hard lessons he's learned in life.

All of this is why I'm honored to introduce you to Coach Brian Goins and his playbook, *Playing Hurt*. I'm confident that if you listen to the Coach and run his plays, you will get into the game and improve your relationship with God, with your wife, and with your children.

So lace 'em up, suit up, and get ready to step up and break a sweat for the game of your life!

DENNIS RAINEY
President of FamilyLife and
host of *FamilyLife Today*

Acknowledgments

TO MY BRIDE— Remember the dream box? One down.

TO BRANTLEY— Never forget . . .
TO PJ— Keep jumping into cold water.
TO GIBBERS— Meet me at the tire swing.

TO MY "AND GUYS"— Jim, Walls, Werner, K-Rant, the Good Doctor, Mets, Elder Hartsock, Knepp, Fite, and Crotts.

TO THE DON— I need huge royalties to repay all those lunches. Your poster looms large on my wall.

TO DAD AND MOM— Thanks for being cycle-breakers and legacy-makers.

TO RENAISSANCE— You wake me up with joy every day.

Chapter 1

Replays

Name your favorite athlete who played hurt. If you're into sports at all, I'll bet someone comes to mind. If not, you can probably find a classic replay on ESPN. Every overproduced pre-Olympic video montage includes sprinter Derek Redmond, at the 1992 Games in Barcelona, limping to the finish line in the 400m on a torn hamstring while he leans on his father for support. You get a little teary eyed whenever you see Kerri Strug nail that vault from the 1996 Olympics—though you would never admit to watching women's gymnastics.

If you're from my parents' generation, you might refer to someone who played hurt by saying, "He pulled a Willis Reed." I had to look the guy up on Wikipedia. Reed, the Hall of Fame center who carried the New York Knicks out of the NBA cellar in the late 1960s, is known for one of the greatest moments in Madison Square Garden history, during the 1970 NBA championship series against the Los Angeles Lakers. Suffering from a torn thigh muscle—an injury suffered in Game 5—Reed stunned the Lakers and fans for both teams by walking onto the court during warm-ups for the deciding Game 7. After conceding the tip-off to Wilt Chamberlain, Reed scored the first two baskets of the game for the Knicks. Though those were the only points he would score that night, his presence on the court inspired his teammates, and they toppled the Lakers 113–99, securing the Knicks' first NBA title.

Not that anyone from Boston would care.

However, any r-dropping Red Sox fan will point to the bloody red sock worn by all-star pitcher Curt Schilling after he ruptured a tendon in his ankle during the 2004 playoffs. His season should have been over, but in an unprecedented move, doctors constructed a wall of stitches around the ruptured tendon, allowing Schilling to pitch twice more in the playoffs. The television announcers spotted blood seeping through Schilling's sock during Game 6 of the American League Championship Series against the hated New York Yankees. He soaked the sock again in Game 2 of the World Series against the St. Louis Cardinals, when his gutsy performance helped to finally put the dreaded Curse of the Bambino to rest as the BoSox won their first championship in eighty-six years.

I'm a fair-weather baseball fan. I love going on dollar hot dog night at a new ballpark designed to look old, but I'm probably not going to watch the game on TV. Basketball is more my passion. Still, I'll never forget the 1988 World Series between the Los Angeles Dodgers and the Oakland Athletics. My dad was the Dodger fan; I just jumped on his bandwagon.

In the bottom of the ninth inning in Game 1, the Dodgers were down 4–3, with two outs and the tying run on first base. Perched on the mound for the Athletics was future Hall of Famer Dennis Eckersley, the quintessential closer, who was known to set down batters in the ninth inning like swatting mosquitoes at a picnic. One out away from a save, he awaited the announcement of a pinch hitter for the Dodgers' pitcher.

Over in the Dodgers' dugout, manager Tommy Lasorda was considering his options. The best hitter he had on the bench was outfielder Kirk Gibson, that season's National League MVP, but Gibson was in no shape to bat. He had been held out of the starting lineup because of injuries to both legs suffered during the National League Championship Series, and on top of that he was sick with a stomach virus. Nevertheless, before the Dodgers came to bat in the ninth, he had sent a message to Lasorda: "I can hit."

Now, with the game on the line, Lasorda sent him to the plate.

Gibson hobbled out of the dugout and immediately fell behind in the count 0–2. After Eckersley missed with his next two pitches, Gibson fouled another one off before working the count to full.

Not wanting to put the go-ahead run on base, Eckersley came with his signature backdoor slider, looking for a strike-out. Gibson took an awkward swing and connected, sending the ball high over the right field wall. Home run! My dad and I jumped up and down like we were in the cheap seats while Gibson, barely jogging, pumped his fist back and forth as he trotted slowly around the bases. The Dodgers went on to win the Series in five games.

No one had to tell me, at age sixteen, "Now Brian, that's a man." Something stirred inside of me. Something ingrained in every man. I wanted that chance. I dreamed of playing hurt and being the hero one day.

For most guys, though, there comes a day when they realize that the closest they'll ever come to playing hurt in a championship game is the day they're home sick from work and making last minute trades in their fantasy league. Nevertheless, you may have some highlight-reel memories of playing through pain in other venues: maybe from the classroom when you pulled an all-nighter to get a paper done. Or maybe in the boardroom when you pushed past your fear and insecurity to challenge a superior. Or maybe you're a man in uniform who took a bullet but kept moving until you got your buddy back to safety. I bet if we shared a cup of coffee together we could find some replays of you playing hurt.

Especially if we started pulling out game film from your dating career.

Sitting in the Freon Zone

My wife, Jen, grew up in northwest Montana, near Glacier National Park. I grew up in suburban northern Virginia, near a swamp they converted into our nation's capital. Not every guy can say this, but for summer vacations, I love going to see my in-laws. Even the founding fathers fled DC in the summer—and if they'd had the choice, I'm sure they would have traveled to the purple mountain majesty where you need a Windbreaker in the shade and no one knows the meaning of the word *humidity*. When I'm in Montana, I always spend a few days writing in one of my favorite coffee shops.

While I was finishing up a chapter for this book, I noticed a young couple off in a corner in the comfy chairs. They weren't sporting any rings and they both looked as if their metabolism was still working at full capacity. I pegged them in their early twenties. The young lady, with arms folded tightly across her chest, leaned over and asked the guy to switch seats with her. I looked up and saw the air conditioning vent pointed right down her neck. As the young guy promptly moved into the Freon zone, I imagined an announcer saying, "Let's watch that again, Bob. *Bam!* Did you see him jump up and dive into that cold blast of air? He knew he was about to be pummeled, but he took the hit anyway."

It reminded me of one of my own replays from when I was pursuing Jen. Long story short, I had chased her all the way to Bangkok, Thailand. (No, I wasn't a stalker.) She was teaching at an international school, and I had taken a year off from graduate school to go on a "mission trip." (You don't have to guess what the true mission was.) In Bangkok, they have three seasons: hot, hotter, and hot and wet. During the rainy season, you don't go anywhere without an umbrella. One night, Jen and I had saved up enough pennies to take a break from chicken fried rice and pad thai to enjoy some American grub. During a deluge worthy of Noah, we donned rain slickers and headed out to Tony Roma's. After a few racks of ribs, we noticed that the rain had finally subsided, and we took that opportunity to catch a cab back to our apartment complex. Jen said good-night, gave me a peck on the cheek, and then said, "Oh, I left my umbrella at the restaurant."

Of course I responded with something soothing like, "Well,

I'm pretty sure they have one at . . . about any store in a three-block radius."

Jen shrugged her shoulders, "Oh well. It was one of my favorites. I loved that pattern."

It was the first time I learned that there are people in this world who notice patterns on umbrellas.

Bangkok has about two major highways for a population of around twelve million. Tony Roma's was on the other side of town. It was a thirty-minute one-way trip and a thirty-dollar round-trip cab fare. We both accepted reality. It was time to play taps for that umbrella.

The next morning, when Jen left for school, she found her favorite patterned umbrella propped up against her door.

"Let's watch that one in slow motion, Bob," the announcer might have said. "Did you see how Brian pump faked and then ran the reverse to snatch victory from the jaws of defeat? What determination! What drive!"

In a related story: On a recent rainy day in Charlotte, as we pulled out of the garage with our three kids to head down to the grocery store, Jen said, "Oh, I left my umbrella on the front porch."

"Don't worry," I said, "I'll get you close enough to the store that you won't get too wet."

"Ouch," says the announcer. "He ran away from that hit like a burglar fleeing a crime scene!"

When the game of romance is on the line, guys are willing to move into the Freon zone or spend thirty bucks in cab fare chasing down a five-dollar umbrella. But when the game shifts to marriage, I've discovered that, most of the time, guys would rather just sit on the bench.

Jen would probably tell you that I still open the door for her, gladly take the cold chair, and usually get the umbrella for her in the rain. (My dad calls that "being a gentleman.") And whether they've grown up in Kalispell, Montana, or Alexandria, Virginia, even married men still practice chivalry. Most guys I know are willing to endure a bit of hardship for their bride and would be more than willing to take a bullet for her in a life-and-death situation. But when it's his bride who fires the bullet—criticizing him for coming home late again from work, disrespecting him in public, or ignoring his advances in private—rather than play through the pain, he'd like to see someone pay for those wounds.

When Jen wounds me with a sarcastic remark or a broken expectation, the last thing I want to do is get back in the game. When my own insecurities hinder me from leading spiritually or resolving a conflict, I want to find a bench—preferably with a big-screen TV. I either want vindication for my injury or I want to escape from my fears. In any case, I don't look up to God and say, "Put me in, Coach. I'm ready to play."

Replays from Scripture

Long before SportsCenter on ESPN, people visualized replays from the written word. In a letter to a young church, the apostle Paul showed "clips" to the congregation about playing through pain as he tried to plant churches:

> As servants of God we commend ourselves in every way: by great endurance, in afflictions, hardships, calamities, beatings, imprisonments, riots, labors, sleepless nights, hunger. . . . We are treated as imposters, and yet are true; as unknown, and yet well known; as dying, and behold, we live; as punished, and yet not killed; as sorrowful, yet always rejoicing; as poor, yet making many rich; as having nothing, yet possessing everything. (2 Corinthians 6:4–5, 8–10)

If only he'd had a camcorder back in the day. What Paul doesn't capture in those clips are the countless times he was wounded by the very people to whom he was writing. We don't know if Paul was ever married, but in many ways his church plants were like brides to him. And those brides fired their share of bullets. From doubting his leadership, to comparing his gifts, to demeaning him in public, they wounded the man who had poured his life into theirs. But rather than pursue vindication, he pursued them. Rather than dwell on his insecurities, he got back in the game. Paul could model perseverance and love because, in his mind, he kept replaying the clip of another classic playing-through-pain moment.

On a hill known as the Skull, Jesus played through the ultimate pain. It had begun twenty-four hours earlier when his closest friends betrayed him. Some had fled, others had lied about knowing him, and one had turned him over to the authorities with a kiss. After being wrongfully accused by three illegal courts, he was stripped, beaten, and scourged with a whip made of multiple cords knotted with bits of metal or bone, designed to lodge in the skin and rip the flesh. The same crowd of people who just days before had shouted praises now spit in his face. Long thorns dug into his forehead as a makeshift "crown" was jammed onto his head. Nails pierced his wrists and feet. As his blood trickled down from the cross, he heaved up and down for hours until he suffocated. During the entire ordeal, his heavenly Father refused to alleviate the pain.

At any moment during the crucifixion, Jesus

→ had the power to fight back;
→ had the right to demand vindication;
→ deserved to be pitied for his wounds.

Instead, he played through.

Why?

The author of the book of Hebrews gives us a clue: "Let us run with endurance the race that is set before us, looking to Jesus, the founder and perfecter of our faith, who for the *joy* that was set before him endured the cross, despising the shame, and is seated at the right hand of the throne of God" (Hebrews 12:1–2, emphasis added). Jesus dug deep because something more was on the line than his body, his rights, and his pride—namely, *us*. More than his own life, Jesus valued you and me.

Paul used this same example when he talked to husbands: "Husbands, love your wives, as Christ loved the church and *gave himself up for her*" (Ephesians 5:25, emphasis added). Jesus endured the wounds inflicted both by his bride and on behalf of his bride, though he was strong enough to fight back, justified enough to be vindicated, and wounded enough to deserve pity. And yet when my own bride, or my insecurities, wound me in my marriage, my first reactions are to fight back, demand justice, and desire sympathy.

If I'm going to dig deep and play hurt, I first have to realize that more is at stake than my body, my rights, or my pride.

When Derek Redmond, Kerri Strug, Willis Reed, Curt Schilling, or Kirk Gibson faced their decisions to sit or suffer through, something overpowered their feelings of pain. It wasn't medication. People play through pain when their passions overpower their feelings. When my heart starts craving something more glorious than my power to retaliate, my desire for vindication, or my hope for pity, I step up. After Paul replayed his personal clips to the church at Corinth, he wrote, "We have spoken freely to you, Corinthians; our heart is wide open. You are not restricted by us, but you are *restricted in your own affections*. In return . . . widen your hearts also" (2 Corinthians 6:11–13, emphasis added). Unlike many pastors, Paul never used guilt to motivate his people to action. Instead, he desired to open up their "restricted" affections. He aimed at expanding their passions more than expanding their lists of *oughts* and *shoulds*. Like a coach shouting from the sideline, he cheered them on: "Be watchful, stand firm in the faith, *act like men, be strong*" (1 Corinthians 16:13, emphasis added). Paul dug into the psyche of the men in the church: Real men play through pain.

In this book, I don't want to guilt-trip you into action. I also don't want to merely offer tips and techniques on being a better husband. Frankly, there are far better marriage coaches out there than I am. More than anything, I want to expand your vision, and I pray that God will open up your restricted passions. I want you to know that you're not alone in the battle. And as you learn to play hurt, I hope you'll discover a few plays you can run to help prevent further injuries.

I hope this book widens your heart and loads some replays into your mind that will capture your soul. When my dad I were watching Kirk Gibson limp around those bases, I was so moved by a man I had never met and never would meet face-to-face.

Baseball's not even my sport, but because of his one sacrificial action, I craved a chance to play with the same passion. I wanted the chance to dig deep.

In the game of marriage, God is not looking for men who will take the air conditioner seat or grab an umbrella. Those acts of chivalry are all well and good, but what God is looking for are husbands who will "act like men" when suffering a deep bruise to their pride, an assault to their ego, or a blow to their expectations.

When you find yourself in the ninth inning, down 4–3, with two outs and the tying run on first, the question is, Will you step up to the plate?

THE HOT SEAT

Welcome to "the hot seat." It's time to answer some questions about your game . . .

1. What are some of your favorite replays of athletes who played hurt?

2. What has been the toughest experience in your life that you had to gut through? What was the result? What did you learn about yourself through that time?

3. When you're wounded by your wife, or by your own insecurities, what is your default response: fight back? demand justice? look for pity? How can you push past your initial reaction and learn to play hurt?

Chapter 2

Posters on Your Wall

WHAT POSTERS DID YOU PUT on your wall as a kid?

Maybe it was #99—Wayne Gretzky, or #16—Joe Montana, or #7—David Beckham, or #51—Randy Johnson. Whether you shot a puck, spiraled a pigskin, slide-tackled a ball, or threw a slider, I bet you emulated someone in your sport. It didn't take long after the invention of the photograph for marketers to capitalize on the hero worship in our culture. From baseball cards to video game covers to posters, young boys over the years have proudly displayed their icons.

For me, it was #23—Michael Jordan. I loved every poster of his, from the 1982 NCAA National Championship–winning shot over Georgetown to his leap in the air after downing the Cleveland Cavaliers with a last-second shot in the 1989 NBA playoffs. But my favorite poster, the one with top billing in my bedroom, was of Michael soaring from the foul line during a slam-dunk competition. Ball extended, tongue out, legs spread, red swoosh on his Nikes. The phrase below read: "Be Like Mike."

And I tried.

I bought the shoes. I stuck out my tongue. I practiced hours every day. I remember how it felt the first time I dunked the ball. I remember when I did a 360 and dunked the ball. I remember when I leapt from the foul line . . . okay, so I'm stretching the truth in that last statement. Okay, okay, so the last three statements are lies. I never leapt from the foul line. I never did a 360. And as hard as I tried, the only hoop I ever dunked on hung from my bedroom door. I put the "can't jump" in "white men can't jump." But even though I couldn't jump as high, shoot as accurately, or play as well as Michael Jordan, I never stopped trying to be like Mike.

For those who didn't grow up during the running of the Chicago Bulls in the '90s, Michael Jordan adorned many a boy's wall for countless reasons: his gravity defying dunks, his silky-sweet jumper, and his ability to create shots for his teammates. But the trait that made him the quintessential basketball player of the twentieth century was his tenacity to win at all costs. I'll never forget watching Game 5 of the 1998 NBA championship series against the hungry Utah Jazz with Karl Malone and John Stockton. Though the Bulls took the first two games, the pendulum swung back to the Jazz in Games 3 and 4. For Game 5, in Salt Lake City, Jordan limped into the arena with a terrible case of the stomach flu. But that didn't seem to diminish his game. Fighting through fever and nausea, Jordan poured in thirty-eight points, including the game-deciding three-pointer in the final minute. As he collapsed in Scottie Pippen's arms at the end of the game, the world sat stunned at his courageous performance. Michael Jordan played through pain.

The Poster Husband

I don't remember much from my wedding day. For me, it was an obligatory ceremony leading up to the real event that night. I recall two things: how much I wanted to get Jen out of her dress, and the pastor saying something about loving my wife like Christ loved the church. Maybe you don't go to church. And maybe you don't know much about the Bible. But if a pastor married you, he probably uttered the same loaded statement. In effect, he slapped a poster of Jesus on your wall. And underneath the picture was a phrase: "Be like Christ." Don't you wish it could have been, "Be like Homer Simpson"?

D'oh!

After watching "game film" on Jesus (reading the four gospels), it's easy to visualize many posters of Christ in action—loving people: breaking bread for hungry followers, placing ignored orphans on his lap, teaching soul-starved people on a hill. Most husbands know innately they should love and provide for their wives. So what sets Jesus apart? What makes him the quintessential man of history? For one, no one played through pain like Jesus. Peter, a friend and follower who traveled with Jesus for three years, pointed out this quality to a young church struggling under the pain of persecution:

> For to this you have been called, because Christ also suffered for you, leaving you an example [in other words, here's your poster], so that you might follow in his steps. . . . When he was reviled, he did not revile in return; when he suffered, he did not threaten, but continued entrusting himself to him who judges justly. He himself bore our sins in his body on the tree. (1 Peter 2:21–24)

Paul refers to this same image in his "playbook for marriage" in Ephesians 5: "Husbands, love your wives, as Christ loved the church *and gave himself up for her*" (verse 25, emphasis added). Paul certainly calls men to care and provide for their wives as we care for our own bodies; but at the forefront, he visualizes a poster of radical sacrifice. The quintessential trait of a good husband is one who plays through pain; someone who willingly sacrifices his ego, self-respect, and his very life for his bride. When reviled, he chooses not to revile in return. When he suffers, he does not threaten. In other words, when the going gets tough, he gets in the game.

To "be like Mike," I needed to soar through the air from the foul line with my tongue hanging out. To "be like Christ," I need to endure nails and thorns. Though I can try to be like Mike every time I pick up a basketball, I can't be like Christ unless I love when I'm wounded, unless I serve after I've been scarred, unless I pursue when someone's running away from me. That's our poster image, the example we're trying to emulate.

It didn't take me long after the wedding to realize how far short of the goal I fell. I remember when I came home late from work—again—with a peace offering of flowers. Jen grabbed them, sighed, threw them on the kitchen table, and said, "You don't get it, do you?" I remember leaving for work the next day with a gnawing pit in my stomach. It wasn't indigestion; it was lack of conflict resolution. Another time, I remember hearing my wife say, "Why is it you pray with other guys, but never pray with me?" And I remember the first time I heard, "Didn't we just make love a couple of days ago?"

I didn't get it. I didn't know how to handle conflict. I didn't pray with my wife. I didn't know why her appetite for sex didn't match mine. And regardless of how many times I saw "Be Like Christ" hanging on the walls of my mind, I never felt as if I had the game to play like that. True, the fact that I never jumped as high or shot as well as Michael Jordan never stopped me from trying to imitate him on the basketball court; but as a wounded husband, I found it easy to quit trying to be like Christ.

I just don't have what it takes to be that kind of husband, I thought.

Regardless of what sport you played—or maybe your game was music, art, drama, chess, computers—you wanted to play like your heroes. What will it take for you to play the game of marriage like the man whose poster the apostle Paul put on the wall for us? It's going to take something more than your instincts and good intentions. In twelve concise verses, Paul presents a playbook for husbands who want to love like Christ loves. If you follow Jesus, you have what it takes to succeed. Husbands, in this chapter, we're asking if you have the guts to "Be Like Christ."

"Goins, You're Stroke!"

When I was a freshman in high school, I clocked in at six-feet-even and maybe a buck thirty soaking wet. That meant many things. For starters, I never caught the eye of any girls or the football coach. Instead, I went out for a sport called *crew*. Because I was a tall, lanky guy, I fit perfectly in a long, skinny boat with seven other guys. On the first day of practice, the coach assembled us eight gangly, knobby-kneed freshmen, looked us over and said, "Goins, you're stroke."

Yes! I'm stroke!

"What's stroke?"

I soon found out that "stroke" was the rower who sat at the back of the boat (really the front, because we rowed backwards) closest to the coxswain (the little munchkin who steered the boat and barked orders) and was responsible for setting the pace and the rhythm for the other rowers. The coxswain kept a stopwatch to time how many strokes per minute we rowed (somewhere between twenty-four and thirty-eight), and he determined when we needed to pick up the pace: "Goins, I've got you at a twenty-four right now; we need to get it up to a thirty-two, let's do a power ten in two strokes . . ."

Four things became very clear to me:

1. I had not been selected because of my skill or experience.
2. I was no better than anyone else in the boat.
3. My two main responsibilities were to listen to the coxswain and set the pace.
4. The key to victory was keeping my eyes in the boat.

Husbands, You Were Not Selected for Your Skill or Your Experience

Think back to your wedding day. Right at the end of the ceremony, when the pastor or judge (or man holding the shotgun) said, "I now pronounce you husband and wife," God looked at your new two-person crew and appointed you as stroke. Contrary to your opinion of yourself (whether overly inflated or severely deflated), it wasn't because of your experience or skill. It was simply because every organization, from boats to boardrooms, needs someone to set the pace. Your wife may be CEO of a Fortune 500 company and you may work in the mailroom;

yet, for whatever reason, God designated you, the husband, as "stroke of the boat."

When my crew coach said, "Goins, you're stroke," he gave me a title and a set of responsibilities even though I had yet to pull an oar. The same thing happened the day you got married. You were given a title (*husband*) and a set of responsibilities (we'll get to those in a minute), even though the only husbandly thing you had done to that point was kiss your bride.

It's one thing to know your title; it's quite another to fulfill the job description. A man with a title but no clear job description can be dangerous. He can turn into an abuser or an abdicator—either misusing power that was never granted or shirking his responsibilities. Abusers are like the boss who mistakes the corporation for his kingdom. Or the quarterback who thinks *captain* means, "Whatever I say, goes." Abdicators are like the teammate who just shrugs his shoulders when he misses an assignment. Or a subcontractor who seems to assume that someone else will come along and fix his shoddy work.

Abusers and abdicators. Equally frustrating, and equally damaging.

As husbands, we can fall into both traps, though we tend to lean one way or the other. But when you watch the game film on Jesus (by reading the four gospels), you'll notice that he never abuses his title and he never abdicates his responsibilities.

So, how are you doing so far? As a husband, do you treat your household like it's your personal kingdom? Or do you abdicate your responsibilities and shrug your shoulders when you miss an assignment? Or are you stroke? (Before you answer too quickly, you may want to ask your bride. Give her the freedom to answer honestly.)

Husbands, You're No Better
Than Anyone Else in the Boat

In crew, just because I had the title of *stroke*, it didn't give me any special standing with my teammates. I didn't get a bigger oar. The number three rower displaced the same amount of water as I did. And if I tried to pull harder or faster than the other rowers, the whole boat suffered. If we won a race, it was because we all rowed in sync.

Husbands who fall into the trap of abusing their title love to quote Scripture. They especially like 1 Peter 3:1, "Wives, be subject to your own husbands," and Colossians 3:18, "Wives, submit to your husbands, as is fitting in the Lord."

Some men like to quote from Paul's playbook on marriage, Ephesians 5:22–23, because it tells wives *why* they are to "be subject" to their husbands: "Wives, submit to your own husbands, as to the Lord. For the husband is the *head* of the wife even as Christ is head of the church" (emphasis added).

Men love titles. Especially those that puff up our chests with assumed authority. Here God calls husbands "the head." For some guys, that means *power*, *position*, or *priority*. Other husbands prefer abdication. They love to call their wives "The Boss." I've also heard many women say, "Well if he's the head, I'm the neck and I turn him any way I want!"

My first problem with husbands quoting Ephesians 5:22 is that Paul is speaking to wives there, not to husbands. Of the thirteen verses in Ephesians directed to couples, nine are addressed to husbands, three are addressed to wives, and the other verse—actually the first verse in the section—says, "submitting *to one another* out of reverence for Christ" (Ephesians 5:21, emphasis added). It seems that husbands ought to be far more concerned about *their own* job description than about what Paul says to their wives.

Though we won't delve here into the heart of submission issues, let's at least be clear on what submission is not: kowtowing, being a doormat, suffering in silence, or being second-rate. Jesus modeled submission in that he "did not count equality with God a thing to be grasped, but made himself nothing, taking the form of a servant" (Philippians 2:6–7). Christian doctrine teaches the mysterious concept of Trinity: one God; three persons; equal essence, but distinct roles. For the Trinity to work, Jesus willingly chose to submit to the authority of the Father. Yet there will come a day when every knee will bow and every tongue will confess that Jesus is Lord (see Philippians

2:10–11). He may be the second person of the Trinity but he's not second-rate or in second place. We will worship him as God, not give him the silver medal. From his example, I define submission as "strength restrained for a purpose," not "strength restrained by a person."

On my crew team, though I had the title of *stroke*, I was no better (or worse) than anyone else in the boat. In my marriage, though I have the title of *husband*, I'm no better or worse than my wife. It's just that, for any organization to work, even marriage, someone has to set the pace.

Husbands, Listen to the Coxswain and Set the Pace

If you're going to be stroke of the boat in your marriage, you should probably know what that entails.

As a novice rower, I learned it meant I sat close enough to the coxswain to smell the burritos on his breath—and he was my primary focus. The coxswain is the only one in the boat who really knows what's going on. The other rowers trust him for direction. As stroke, I never turned around and barked out orders to the boat. My job was to respond to what he said and adjust my rowing to what he said. When he shouted a command, I never said,

→ "Man, I'm bushed right now, I'm going to lift my oar out of the water. Can you tell the other guys to pick up the pace?"

→ "Listen, when these guys start pulling their weight, I'll start digging deep."

→ "I'm not nearly as good as other guys. I just don't think I have what it takes."

I might have been stroke of the boat, but I wasn't calling the shots. My relationship with the coxswain worked best—and the whole boat succeeded—when he commanded and I obeyed. If he told me to get the pace up to a thirty-two, I complied. If he told me to back off, I backed off. When he yelled, I responded, regardless of how I felt. I was under submission.

In the same way, in my role as husband, I may be head of the marriage, but I'm not calling the shots. If there's a king in the castle, it's not me. My relationship with God works best—and my marriage succeeds—when God commands and I obey.

So, when I feel irritated, insecure, or intimidated in my marriage, and I hear God's commands—"Don't let the sun go down on your anger. Love her like Christ loved the church. Sanctify her with the word"—I had better not say (as I so often want to),

→ "I've put in a hard day of work today. I don't have the energy to deal with this conflict. Besides, I want to watch SportsCenter."

→ "Listen, when she starts putting out in the bedroom, I'll start pursuing her romantically."

→ "I don't even know what to pray. She's better praying solo."

God calls us as husbands to set the pace in our homes. That includes the spiritual atmosphere, conflict resolution, romance—you name it. If we focus more on our pain than on God's commands, if we'd rather sit on the bench than get in the game, our marriages are not going to work. Both husbands and wives are called to submit in order for the marriage team to function. God commands wives to restrain their strength, even when it hurts. God calls husbands to dig deep and set the pace, even when it hurts.

Husbands, Keep Your Eyes in the Boat

The first rule in rowing is to keep your eyes in the boat. If you're stroke, keep your eyes on the coxswain. If you're one of the other rowers, pretend your eyes are lasers and bore a hole through the neck of the guy in front of you. When you cock your head to the side, you lose power. You're not on a cruise; you're part of a crew.

I'll never forget our freshman state championships. We knew we faced stiff competition from two of the boats, but the third boat we had beaten as if they had left a rower on the dock. In the last 100 meters of the final, we were in third place, just slightly off the pace. Our coxswain screamed out, "Power ten in two!" We dug deep. My rubbery legs pushed through the pain.

As we neared the finish line, we heard a loud crack. I cocked my head to the left. The two boats slightly ahead of us had clashed oars! They were out of the race! Our coxswain pounded the gunwales and screamed, "Eyes in the boat!" And then it was over.

In the last few meters of the race, our two main competitors had taken each other out. But when every rower in our boat looked left, the sudden loss of power enabled the third boat to cruise past us and beat us by half a second. All because we took our eyes out of the boat.

Bad things happen when you take your eyes out of the boat. Our greatest struggles in marriage happen because we look at everyone and everything except Jesus. We look at our bruised egos. We analyze why we're right and she's wrong. We compare our marriages to others that "have it together." But we lose power when we focus outside the boat. The author of Hebrews tells us that we should be "fixing our eyes on Jesus, the author and perfecter of faith" (Hebrews 12:2 NASB). I've discovered I'd much rather try to fix Jen than fix my eyes on Jesus.

I would never hang a poster of Michael Jordan on my wall if I hadn't watched him play. It was his example, which the posters depicted, that I wanted to emulate. As a husband, you know you're supposed to love like Christ; but do you have any idea how Christ loved? Do you watch his game film? Do you sit close enough to him to pick up on his commands? If you've never spent much time focused on Jesus, check out his highlight reel in the first four books of the New Testament (Matthew, Mark, Luke, and John). You'll start to get the picture right away.

When you fix your eyes on Jesus, you'll learn that "headship" has far more to do with *responsibility* and *accountability* than it does with *position* and *authority*. When you fix your eyes on Jesus, you'll be less concerned with the distraction of trying to fix your wife and more concerned about setting the proper pace and rhythm in your own home—which leads to the wins we all desire in marriage: genuine intimacy, good companionship, and spiritual connectedness.

The Wedding Derby

I don't know what your wedding day was like, but I'm guessing it was a blur. In some respects, weddings are like the Kentucky Derby—months of anticipation and preparation for an event that gallops by in about two minutes. Or so it seems. We spend countless hours and dollars finding just the right dress, just the right flowers, and just the right food. We invite our friends and family, and they crowd the rail to get the best view of the happy couple. The minister prattles on with the precision of a track announcer as the bride and groom are put through their paces. Then, after a photo finish, and a kiss, they run off with the roses.

Every now and again, I have the privilege of officiating at a wedding. I hope when people leave the ceremony they don't feel as if they've been to the Derby! I see it more as an art class. Now, I'm not an art guy. I can't tell you if Manet is better than Monet. But Paul describes the union of husband and wife like the painting of a masterpiece. He says of a man and a woman joined as one flesh, "This mystery is profound, and I am saying that it refers to Christ and the church" (Ephesians 5:32). In other words, a marriage is an earthly painting of a spiritual reality.

Like I said, I'm not an art guy, but friends who go to museums tell me it takes time to appreciate fine art. So, at weddings, I take my time appreciating God's brushstrokes. See how God blends two distinct hues—male and female—into one beautiful color. Notice how he ghosts the image of Jesus and the church in the shadows of husbands and wives. If you compare the wedding ceremony to a canvas, by the end an image emerges for the husband to emulate. I challenge the groom by calling him to

→ Lead in such a way so that when his wife submits to him it will be a joy more than a chore.
→ Love his wife in such a way that she never doubts his devotion to her.
→ Sacrifice in such a way that when his wife thinks of Christ, she sees her husband's face.

Don't worry, though; I'm realistic. I'm fairly certain that the only thing the groom remembers is that he couldn't wait to get his bride out of her dress, and that the pastor said something about "loving your wife as Christ loved the church." That's why, when the couple gets back from their honeymoon, they discover a bound, personalized copy of the wedding message in their mailbox. And every year, on their anniversary date, I pick up the phone and give the husband a call to catch up and deliver a not-so-subtle reminder: "Remember, you pledged before God, your wife, your family, your friends, and me to 'be like Christ.'"

That kind of love takes guts. After the honeymoon is but a memory, what motivates a man to love like that?

A Husband's Crib Sheet for Playing Hurt

If you watch football you've noticed the quarterback look at something in the huddle—a wide laminated card affixed to his wrist. It sums up a team's huge playbook in a series of codes. At the end of almost every chapter we are going to build our own "code" that sums up Paul's Playbook for husbands. By the end you will have the essence of this book in five signature phrases. You may not want to strap it to your wrist, but sliding it into your pocket may not hurt. You can also use the questions at the end of each chapter for a small group or to propel you personally into action.

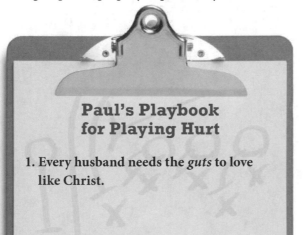

**Paul's Playbook
for Playing Hurt**

1. Every husband needs the *guts* to love like Christ.

THE HOT SEAT

1. If you were to put a poster on your wall of the greatest husband you know, who would it be? Why?

2. Pick a character in popular culture that most resembles a sacrificial husband. Explain your choice.

3. Which responsibilities have you abdicated in your marriage? Which ones do you abuse?

4. Are you watching any game film on Jesus? Why or why not? What is one thing you can do this week to keep your eyes in the boat and focused on Jesus?

Chapter 3

The Motivation to Play Hurt

WHY DO YOU LOVE YOUR WIFE?

Don't think too hard; just jot down your answers in the margin . . .

I'm going to wager you picked from one of two general themes. Either you love her because of something she does for you: She's beautiful. She's funny. She makes me feel strong. She always lifts me up. She's godly. She's good in the sack.

Or you love her because it's expected: I know it's the right thing to do. It's what God expects of me. I look at her and think, "WWJD: What would Jesus do?"

Perhaps it's a mixture of both. The first motivation capitalizes on her *performance*. The second focuses more on your *obligation*. Both reasons are common. Both motivations eventually run out of steam.

The Big Day

You remember the day. The big day. The day that people had planned for and looked forward to for months.

Men milled about in tuxedos. Long lost family members

appeared out of nowhere. Friends whispered jokes and slapped backs. Cameras flashed. Butterflies swirled. Champagne flowed. The anticipation mounted. Lofty promises were made.

The music swirled to a crescendo. Then the officiant turned to the audience and uttered the immortal words, "With the fifth pick, the Washington Redskins select . . ."

Draft day.

So much pomp surrounding so much uncertainty. Remind you of anything?

Soon draft day turns into training camp. Potential must now translate into measurable performance. Regardless of all the draft day hoopla, players must now make their blocks, run their patterns, and catch the ball. It's time to put up or shut up.

Making a big splash in the draft doesn't guarantee a great future. It seems as if every year a few "stars of tomorrow" crash and burn. The playmaker guaranteed to unify the locker room is traded because of bad chemistry. The franchise player loses a step or picks up a nagging injury, and the spotlight turns into a spot on the bench.

In sports, when we don't perform, everyone forgets about draft day. And rightly so. Applause is meted out based on merit. Sports are just as ruthless as school or business. No one cares about good intentions. It's about execution on the field.

In sports, a focus on performance is fine. In marriage, it's deadly.

As men, we often believe our marriages would be better if our wives would only *perform* better. Our applause and affection is meted out not based on our original lofty promises—for richer, for poorer, in sickness and health, in good times and bad . . . till death do us part—but on what our wives say and do.

Did she pull her weight today?

Did she perform in the bedroom?

Did she respect me in front of my friends last night?

Did she keep track of her spending this month?

I would love her more if she would just _____.

And when she doesn't measure up, we forget all about the wedding day hoopla.

Performance can be defined as anything our wives must *do* or *say* in order for us to be content in our marriage. We start acting like those coaches in training camp, running around with clipboards, jotting down every missed tackle, dropped ball, or lapse of passion. In order to fix our marriages, we start believing that we—or someone else—must fix our wives.

We couldn't be more wrong.

From Performance to Faith

One thing I've noticed about performance-based relationships: they don't have a strong track record. If we reserve the right to pull out or sit on the bench when our wives don't measure up to our standards or when things don't go as planned, we will. God did not design marriage like a car—time to trade it in after 36,000 miles. He wants us to take our eyes off of our immediate circumstances—how things are going, according to our own plans and expectations—and to focus them on him. He wants us to move from *performance*-based relationships to *faith*-based relationships.

We discover the winning formula in Hebrews 11:6, where the author makes an audacious claim about God: "Without faith it is impossible to please him, for whoever would draw near to God must believe that he exists and that he rewards those who seek him."

I think that most Christian men would like the inside track on how to please God. Hebrews says we please him by our faith, which is defined as "the assurance of things hoped for, the conviction of things not seen" (Hebrews 11:1). So when we come into relationship with God, we look beyond our present circumstances to the hope of a future glory, with the conviction and assurance that God is able to do what he promised (see Romans 4:21).

Few things embody hope like a wedding day. We make lofty promises about countless unforeseen variables. Would you have paused on your wedding day if you had seen a few snapshots from your future?

→ Your wife with twenty-five extra pounds, stretch marks, and hair in some unusual places
→ Your budget after you've been laid off for six months
→ Your wife as a terminally ill patient
→ Your pain when you discover that your wife has cheated on you

Lofty promises mean little on draft day. They only matter when they're tested on the field. To play through pain and bad performance requires faith. But God doesn't ask you to commit to your relationship with him without a corresponding hope. And that same hope applies to marriage. When you put your faith in God and seek him first—rather than focusing on your wife's *performance*—he will reward you by guaranteeing that your marriage will sustain the hardest of trials and the worst of performances. Loving by faith doesn't come naturally. As we'll see in chapter 8, it requires a power we don't possess.

On the other hand, when you finally realize that your love for your bride can't be based on performance, if you don't swing the pendulum toward *faith*, the alternative is to settle for a lesser—and much more frustrating—motive: *obligation*.

A Bad Case of the Oughts

Like most fortysomething, red-blooded, Christian husbands, Ron figured out that having a child or two dramatically changes a marriage. His wife didn't regain her youthful figure or match his desire for sexual intimacy. Routines developed. Meeting his needs dropped somewhere between the kids and the pets. So Ron recalibrated his expectations in order to enjoy a predictable, comfortable, suburban life.

Then Ron's wife developed an unidentified illness that caused great fatigue, loss of strength, and a more severely reduced libido. Suddenly, Ron's predictable—albeit lowered—expectations of life took a further turn south.

But Ron was determined to love his wife. After all, that's what Christian husbands do. Just as Christ had died for the church, Ron knew that he *ought* to die to himself. So he tried. After a year of loving out of obligation, Ron's passion for God and for his marriage began to diminish. He felt more energized away from home. His relationship with his wife teetered between the slim hope of change and the bitterness of busted expectations.

What gives Ron the motivation to love his bride when there's virtually no hope of his "needs" being met in the foreseeable future? He listens to the pastor at the men's event cry out, "Man up! Stop your whining! Love like Christ!" But he feels more guilt than hope. She may never be the companion she once was. She may never fire up her passion in the bedroom again. She may never match his zest for life. So Ron digs deep. He hunts for help. Maybe he downloads a book on marriage. Perhaps he decides to go to a conference. If he's lucky, he won't run into a speaker like me.

A Swift Kick Right Where It Hurts

Guilt drives many guys to marriage counseling or conferences. I see countless Rons in the audience whenever I speak at a marriage conference. From the podium, I see wives sitting with elbows cocked, ready to fire a volley into their husband's gut if he needs to write down a tip. Some of the men have come willingly; others with a gun to their backs. Some have come looking for a spark to rekindle the flame or for shortcuts to restore intimacy. Others have come knowing it's a last resort. Almost all leave with a wheelbarrow full of "to-dos"—listen more, communicate more, initiate date nights, write surprise e-mails, become bilingual in their wife's love language, do more, be more, feel more, pray more, cuddle more. Most men sit in these sessions slumped under the burden of past guilt and future obligation.

As a conference speaker and counselor, I'm a firm believer in getting help for marriages in trouble. But I changed my focus after a guy like Ron approached me at a conference following a split session in which I had talked with the husbands while Jen talked with the wives. He smiled as he shook my hand and gave me a cartoon. On one panel, it showed the women coming out of their session smiling, laughing, and loving the opportunity for girl talk. The second panel showed the men walking out of their session in pain, bent over, covering their privates.

I realized that, for the past hour, I had heaped on even more guilt. Though I had used Paul's playbook from Ephesians 5, with every point clearly drawn from Scripture, the effect on my audience had been like a knee to the groin. I realized I was telling men to sacrifice themselves for their wives like Jesus died for the church, without telling them *why* Jesus sacrificed himself. As husbands, we need to see our role in marriage as a high calling. We need something to carry us past our *obligation*, past our *responsibility*, to a vision of glory that takes our eyes off of our fears and selfish desires. Just as soldiers don't dive on grenades because they *ought* to, and athletes don't come off the bench in excruciating pain because it's the right thing to do, husbands can't be expected to sacrifice themselves out of a sense of duty. We need a higher purpose.

Glory Days

What inspires men to action? Down through the ages, stirring speeches have buried their talons into the hearts of men. Even the most bored teenager in English Lit perks up when he hears the St. Crispin's Day speech in Shakespeare's *Henry V*:

> From this day to the ending of the world,
> But we in it shall be remembered—
> We few, we happy few, we band of brothers;
> For he to-day that sheds his blood with me
> Shall be my brother.[1]

Then he stuffs his English book in his backpack and heads to the locker room to suit up for the night's game, when coaches who can't even pronounce "iambic pentameter" will nevertheless stir their troops with the same vigor as King Henry by screaming to the defense on a fourth and one: *"No guts, no glory!"*

I always pause in my channel surfing if I ever run across William Wallace's speech from *Braveheart*—the one in which he challenges a motley group of vastly outnumbered Scottish farmers standing against battle-hardened British troops on the fields of Stirling. I never get tired of hearing the rogue warrior Wallace turn the tide of cowardice into intrepid courage: "Aye, fight and you may die. Run and you'll live . . . at least awhile. And dying in your beds, many years from now, would you be willing to trade all the days, from this day to that, for one chance, just one chance, to come back here and tell our enemies that they may take our lives, but they'll never take OUR FREEDOM!"

From classic movies to classic sports stations, men relish and relive the moments made eternal by heart-inspiring sacrifices. But we don't need high-dollar Hollywood productions in order to pass down our stories. Just go to Main Street USA, jump into a barber's chair, and listen to the embellished yarns of high school legends. You'll inevitably hear someone say, "Those were the *glory* days." In Scripture, *glory* means "weight." Stories of glory, from Shakespeare's speeches to goal-line stands, create a weight in a man's heart pushing him to do, to live, to act, and to sacrifice. Men discover their courage—their guts—for glory.

One would hope that a husband would feel the weight of glory on his wedding day. Unfortunately, for the tuxedo-clad groom, the glory all falls on the bride. That's why there's no *Groom* magazine. We dress the bride like a princess; we dress the groom like a penguin. At best, he's a footnote; at worst, overlooked. Throughout the day, married veterans remind the rookie that his glory days are long past. They chide the naive husband, "It's all downhill from here!" or "How's the ankle feel? The one with the ball and chain!" or "You just traded in your life for a wife!"

For a man, the wedding day feels more like the finish line than the starting blocks. The glory was getting his bride down the aisle. Then he wakes up one morning and wonders, *What happens next? What's the next hill to climb? Where's the next trophy to win? the next battle to fight? the next goal to achieve? Why do I love this woman? Is it just about sticking it out until one of us dies? Where is the glory in something so ordinary?*

If there was glory in marriage, it seems to fade along with your metabolism. So men tend to pursue glory in everything *but* marriage: securing that untouchable client for their company, pushing everything else aside to hit that deadline, playing on a bum knee in the office softball league, coaching their kids to future glory. Some men exchange real glory for the false allure of lust. They entertain the advances of an attractive woman. They rekindle an old flame on Facebook. They resort to the illusion of intimacy in the form of pornography. Such pursuits tempt men with glory, yet deliver futility.

We retell so few glory stories in marriage. Popular culture paints glowing pictures of winning the girl, but few portraits of loving a wife for a lifetime. The fleeting glory of the wedding is big business, but the lasting glory of marriage is all but ignored. No one replays game film on the husband who pursues a wife who never desires him sexually. No one celebrates the husband who cares for his terminally ill wife. No one pins a medal on the husband who perseveres with a nagging, overweight wife who struggles with depression. And when men don't feel the *glory*, they often won't find the *guts* to dig deep.

Last-Second Shots

The scenarios changed, but the results were always the same.

Every day after school on the neighbor's sloped driveway, you'd find me alone practicing last-second shots. Sometimes my "team" was down by 20 and I staged an unbelievable comeback ending with a turnaround jump shot for three. Sometimes I was on the foul line with no time on the clock: one to tie, the second to win. If I missed the first I always called a lane violation on the "other team." As a boy, no one taught me to crave glory. And even if your childhood passion wasn't a sport, you dreamed of glory in some venue.

I'm not sure we ever grow out of a desire for our name and our fame. And while we may never hear our name chanted in a stadium, it's easy to feel the weight of glory when we excel at work, or reach an impossible goal, or relive the "glory days" when we're down 3–2 in the bottom of the ninth and hit the game-winning homer in the church softball league. Where are those moments in marriage?

Every time I walked over to the neighbor's driveway, I stepped into an arena where it was about my fame and my name. Throughout life I stepped into other venues—from college to graduate school to various jobs—but my craving for glory never changed. On my wedding day I swelled with pride as I saw others gazing at Jen when she appeared in her dress: "Yeah, that's right, I won the girl!" But whether I realized it or not, when Jen and I walked down the aisle as Mr. and Mrs. Goins, I had just stepped into an arena reserved for God's fame and his name. At the beginning of this chapter, did you happen to write "God's glory" in the margin as a reason you love your wife? As we head back to Paul's playbook on marriage we discover when a husband chooses to love despite a wife's performance or his unmet expectations, in some way, it shines the light on God's name and his fame. For that to happen, the boy who walked over to the neighbor's sloped driveway craving glory must die.

Boyish Love vs. Manly Love

You might have heard the phrase, "When I was a child, I spoke like a child, I thought like a child, I reasoned like a child. When I became a man, I gave up childish ways" (1 Corinthians 13:11). You'd think Paul wrote this phrase after his call to "act like men" (1 Corinthians 16:13–14). Instead it comes after the passage you generally see on girly greeting cards: 1 Corinthians 13:4–7. Yeah, the love verses:

> Love is patient and kind; love does not envy or boast; it is not arrogant or rude. It does not insist on its own way; it is not irritable or resentful; it does not rejoice at wrongdoing, but rejoices with the truth. Love bears all things, believes all things, hopes all things, endures all things.

"Love" in our culture is like WD-40. We spray it on everything: I love burgers; I love the Cowboys; I love my wife. Hopefully my love for Jen means more than my love for cooked cow or grown men tackling each other. Paul indicates there came a time in his life when he grew out of an immature, boyish love and embraced a mature, manly love. Every husband who wants to love like Christ must let the boy die.

Boys retaliate quickly when hurt; manly love is patient and kind.

Boys require constant affirmation; manly love is not arrogant or rude.

Boys stew, stammer, and hold grudges when they don't get their way; manly love does not insist on its own way; it is not irritable or resentful.

Boys try to win every argument; manly love does not rejoice at wrongdoing, but rejoices with the truth.

Boys have a short fuse; manly love bears all things.

Boys write people off when wronged; manly love believes God's best for the relationship.

Boys lose hope after they're hurt; manly love always hopes for reconciliation regardless of the pain.

Boys expect to be served; manly love endures all things.

Boys love things that bring them glory; godly men love to bring God glory. When we look back at Ephesians 5, we see how manly love shines the light on God's fame and his name:

> Husbands, love your wives, as Christ loved the church and gave himself up for her, that he might sanctify her, having cleansed her by the washing of water with the word, so that he might present the church to himself in splendor, without spot or wrinkle or any such thing, that she might be holy and without blemish. In the same way husbands should love their wives as their own bodies. He who loves his wife loves himself. . . . This mystery is *profound,* but I am saying that it refers to Christ and the church. (Ephesians 5:25–28, 32, emphasis added)

Most pastors don't have enough time during the wedding ceremony to unveil the mystery of marriage; yet, for Paul, it's the climax of the entire passage. The Greek word for *profound* is *megas*, which connotes "great, mighty, powerfully affecting the senses, and highly esteemed for its excellence."[2] Contrary to how marriage is often perceived in our culture, Paul calls the union between a husband and a wife anything but ordinary. Rather, it's the *visual symbol of an eternal reality.* In a sense, when a husband loves his wife as Christ loves the church, the marriage becomes a living display of God's glory to a watching world. When I concentrate more on setting the pace in my marriage than on measuring my wife's performance, it brings God fame. When a guy like Ron faithfully cherishes his wife as long as she's debilitated, it mysteriously celebrates God's name. How's that for a higher purpose? How's that for a noble calling?

If we sat down with Paul in the barbershop on Main Street, he'd tell us a couple stories of how Jesus loves his bride for God's glory.

Glory Story One: To Beautify the Bride

I remember talking with an older couple about the secret to maintaining intimacy after forty years of marriage and four kids. The wife, Sally, who was in her mid sixties at the time, piped up immediately: "Don still thinks I'm beautiful, even though I know what I look like in the mirror." Her husband had learned the secret of reflecting his wife's beauty back to her so she could see it—and, more importantly, so she could *feel* it.

Men love shiny gadgets. We crave the latest and greatest. So when the shine wears off a man's bride, it's no wonder he silently pines for an upgrade. If he doesn't actively pursue the latest model, he secretly hopes his wife will change. He may even offer some not-so-subtle hints:

"Did you work out today?"

"Are you really going to eat that entire hot fudge sundae?"

"Remember when you wore a bikini?"

A man loves a beautiful bride. Jesus loves to beautify his bride. Catch the difference? Most husbands simply love what is—what they can see. Jesus loves what could be, and he draws forth his bride's inner beauty. Whenever you see the word *sanctify* in Scripture, it means to "set apart" or "make holy." In theological terms, when God "sanctifies" believers, he makes us blameless and holy. It's a lifelong transformation based on God's vow to his people, not based on his people's performance (see Exodus 31:13; Philippians 1:6). Jesus pledges a transforming love that sets his bride apart and makes her beautiful.

When a man loves based on performance, he will expect his wife to stay or become beautiful. When a man loves like Jesus, he will beautify his wife as time passes, regardless of her physical body's natural decline. In Ephesians 5:25, Paul talks of Jesus washing and cleansing his bride. The imagery is drawn from the ceremonial bath that Jewish brides took before the wedding. As a student of the law and the prophets, who had memorized chunks of the Hebrew Scriptures, Paul no doubt saw Ezekiel 16:8–14 zoom through his mind:

> When I passed by you again and saw you, behold, you were at the age for love, and I spread the corner of my garment over you and covered your nakedness; I made my vow to you and entered into a covenant with you, declares the Lord GOD, and you became mine. Then I bathed you with water and washed off your blood from you and anointed you with oil. I clothed you also with embroidered cloth and shod you with fine leather. I wrapped you in fine linen and covered you with silk. And I adorned you with ornaments and put bracelets on your wrists and a chain on your neck. And I put a ring on your nose and earrings in your ears and a beautiful crown on your head. Thus you were adorned with gold and silver, and your clothing was of fine linen and silk and embroidered cloth. You ate fine flour and honey and oil. You grew exceedingly beautiful and advanced to royalty. And your renown went forth among the nations because of your beauty, for it was perfect through the splendor that I had bestowed on you, declares the Lord GOD.

Notice how God's bride blossoms after the wedding day and becomes more beautiful and splendid over time, not because she "worked out" or "aged gracefully," but because God loved her into radiance. If a man views the wedding day as the height of his bride's beauty, then he will never love like Jesus. He'll constantly be comparing what *was* rather than anticipating his role in *what it could be*. No makeup can make up for a husband's lack of love. Facials can only brighten a woman's complexion, not her countenance. For Jesus, the wedding day was simply the start of a lifelong extreme makeover designed to advance his bride to royalty.

Furthermore, Israel wasn't chosen by God because she was impressive; in fact, quite the opposite (see Deuteronomy 7:6–7). In our society, which defines beauty according to the image of airbrushed and augmented blonde bombshells, a wife can wither away under the constant pressure to defy age and gravity—that is, unless her husband helps to draw out and develop her true beauty, which is seen in character, excellence, and wisdom (see Proverbs 31:10–31).

A woman's beauty will either be reflected in a mirror or by her husband. The first is fleeting, the second is forever. In chapters 6 and 7, we'll see how a man can beautify his wife. Our purpose here is simply to capture the vision.

I spend most summers in a small town in Montana. On certain nights, down at the Dairy Queen, you can catch the local hot rod show. If you've ever been to an antique car show, you've seen the results of countless hours spent polishing, buffing, upgrading, and retooling vehicles that otherwise would have been lost to rust and decay. You've marveled at the glory of a fully restored '57 Chevy with shiny overhead cams, or a cherry red '66 Mustang fastback with a glass pack muffler. The owners sacrificed time, energy, emotion, frustration, and money to beautify what was destined for the scrap heap. Why? For the glory of parading their refurbished beauties before a crowd of people eating Dilly Bars. Don't get me wrong; I love polished chrome as much as the next guy. But if we husbands aren't careful, we will spend countless hours, resources, and effort beautifying stuff that fades away, such as cars, instead of pouring energy into the eternal—the woman God gave us. A husband brings God fame when he loves his wife into beauty.

Glory Story Two: A Reverse Wedding

Paul says that Jesus loves and beautifies his Bride because one day he'll parade her in all her intended glory, "that he might present the church to himself in splendor, without spot or wrinkle or any such thing" (Ephesians 5:27). Maybe it sounds weird for Jesus to present something to himself, but when you understand God as Trinity, you see that Paul is painting a picture of the glory of a future wedding—one in which Jesus' bride, the church, will be presented before God the Father. Jesus' constant and sacrificial love wipes away blemishes and smoothes over wrinkles—not out of obligation, but in anticipation of the eventual union of a spotless Bride with a spotless Lamb in the presence of the Father (see Revelation 19:6–9).

Cleaning This Gun

I think that every dad who gets a new daughter should be issued a shotgun upon leaving the hospital. As the dad of a daughter myself, I know that one day some sixteen-year-old, pimply faced, hormonally charged punk will come knocking on my door to take my daughter on a date. As he looks my little treasure up and down with his lusty eyes, he'll be too distracted to see what's in my eyes. He won't know that my favorite naps were spent with my baby daughter nestled against my chin. That I spent a fortune on an American Girl doll just to see her smile on Christmas. That, on countless nights, I prayed with her and rubbed her back until she fell asleep. That I called her Beautiful every day of her life so that, regardless of how the world might judge her, she would always know that she's a beauty in Daddy's eyes. And he probably won't realize that I would go to prison before I would allow his grubby hands to plunder my treasure.

I know of a dad with a brood of daughters, who had a unique way of getting the attention of any young man who came calling on one of his girls. Before the boy drove off with his precious jewel, the dad made him promise to honor, respect, and cherish his daughter. After the boy said, "Yeah, sure, Mister," the dad pulled out a Sharpie and a Louisville Slugger. "Great," he replied, "then you won't mind autographing my bat before you go out. I'll be here waiting for you when you get back . . . with my bat."

Country singer Rodney Atkins wrote a song about sitting down with his daughter's date. He chitchats for a minute or two. Makes the young suitor feel comfortable. He asks the boy what time they'll be home. He reminds him to respect his little treasure. Right before they head out on their date, Rodney sings: "Hey y'all run along and have some fun, I'll see you when you get back. Bet I'll be up all night. Still cleanin' this gun."

Let me dare you to do something. When you see your wife today, take a moment to look longingly into her eyes. Don't say a word; just stare into her eyes: trust me, it will freak her out. Etched on her pupils you will discover two words from God: *My treasure*. Jesus says in Matthew 22:30 that marriage will come to an end in heaven. (But that doesn't mean we tell our wives we need to get all the sex we can here on earth!) Husbands, we need to realize that one day our wives will cease to be our brides. But they will never cease to be God's daughters. The Father—who knitted them together (Job 10:11), wove them in the womb (Psalm 139:13), picked their hair color and numbered every strand (Matthew 10:30), formed every feature, created every personality quirk, and set good works before them to walk in (Ephesians 2:10)—cares more for his daughters than you and I ever could. And he can't wait to see his precious daughters again. One day, the Father will be waiting on the front porch for us to bring his girls back from our decades-long dates. In a weird way, I believe he'll be polishing a gun or toting a Louisville Slugger. If the "head" of the relationship (that's you and me, boy—see Ephesians 5:23) did not beautify his bride into her intended glory, then "heads" will roll. In heaven, Jesus will parade his Bride in all her restored glory. What about you?

Another Wedding Day

When I married Jen, I had no idea of the profoundly deep feelings her father had for his daughter. I was lost in my self-absorbed thoughts. I cared about how Jen made me feel—which was drunk with love and more than a little horny. No doubt her dad wondered how a naive, hormonally charged twenty-four-year-old punk could possibly treasure his daughter as he had all those years. I remember standing at the altar with tears flowing down my face when Jen walked toward me in radiating glory. In that moment, I never imagined that one day she will be part of another, far more glorious, wedding. In that day, I will not be receiving Jen, but handing her back to her heavenly Father. I believe he will ask me, as a steward of what he has given me, "After all these years, what did you do with the treasure I loaned you?" And he'll already know if Jen has been polished or plundered.

Men dig deep when glory is on the line. From the football field to the battlefield to the corporate trenches, men are motivated to play hurt if they feel the weight of glory. As husbands, how can we love our wives in such a manner over a lifetime? There's a reason why Paul's playbook for husbands is about three times longer than his playbook for wives. We don't just need guts and glory; we need serious help. In every battle for glory a cunning enemy rises up. And contrary to popular opinion, that enemy is not your wife.

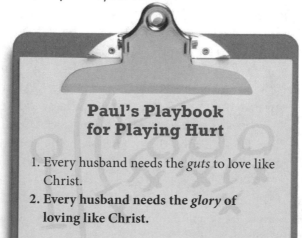

Paul's Playbook for Playing Hurt

1. Every husband needs the *guts* to love like Christ.
2. **Every husband needs the *glory* of loving like Christ.**

THE HOT SEAT

1. What is your main motive for loving your bride? Would you say it leans toward her performance or toward your obligation?

2. Read 1 Corinthians 13:4–7. Look over Paul's description of "manly love." What circumstances tempt you to act more like a boy than a man toward your wife?

3. How do you view Jesus' motives for loving his Bride as different than yours? In what ways did he beautify his bride?

4. Have you ever imagined presenting your bride back to God? How does that change your perspective on how you act toward her now?

Chapter 4

The Real Enemy

"I'VE COMMITTED TWO AFFAIRS in the last year," Jason said.

"Why?" I asked him.

"I don't know. I just let myself get emotionally attached to someone at work."

About twelve inches away, Jason's wife, Kristy, sat in a different galaxy. I asked her, "Why are you here?"

"Because we still want to make this marriage work."

Adultery can strike mortal blows to marriage. Though God hates divorce, even Jesus gave permission in cases of habitual philandering. After a few counseling sessions, I found out how Jason and Kristy had hurt each other over the years, and where they took their pain. Jason's response was to sink into himself, like a player who has just fouled out sulking at the end of the bench. In his eyes, Kristy's performance had waned. She had "let herself go." Eventually, the call of duty to love his wife wasn't enough to overcome his emotional attachment to an attractive woman he met on a business trip. He gave in.

I asked Jason and Kristy if they had a game plan for getting through this. I asked them why God designed marriage. I asked them what they thought a marriage needed to flourish. They had plenty of expectations, but no real answers. The good news:

they still had the desire to stay in the game. I recommended they invest three days and go to a marriage conference.

You Can't Stay in the Locker Room

At the end of most marriage conferences I teach, I play the closing scene from *The Story of Us*. It's a poignant moment that amounts to a halftime locker-room talk when you're down by three touchdowns. Ben and Katie Jordan (played by Bruce Willis and Michelle Pfeiffer) are ready to call it quits. They've been married for fifteen years, but over time the soul mates have turned into roommates. As their teenagers are away at summer camp, they spend the week contemplating whether or not they should end their marriage, and how to break the news to their kids. Initially, they agree not to go to Chow Funs, their classic family go-to restaurant when nothing else sounds good. Chow Funs holds far too many memories.

The scene opens with Ben and Katie standing in a parking lot. As their kids jump into the car, Katie looks at Ben and says, "I say Chow Funs." Ben retorts, "Are you saying Chow Funs because you can't face the kids? Because if that's why you're saying Chow Funs, then don't say Chow Funs!" Katie responds, "No, I'm saying Chow Funs because we are an *us*. There's a history here and histories don't happen overnight." She continues with a locker-room speech that would've made Vince Lombardi proud. She prattles on for three minutes about why she and Ben can't just give up on their marriage. Ben, like most men, waits for her to take a breath. As Katie's speech winds down, the background music swells louder, tickling our emotions until, in tears, Katie says, "I say Chow Funs because I love you!" Ben comes out of his catatonic state, jumps up and down, and runs to the car to tell the kids they're heading to Chow Funs. All the wives in the audience weep and all the guys act like dust mites have invaded their pupils.

I wonder if audiences would respond the same way if the producers took out the background music from that scene. What if the actors hadn't practiced the lines before they spoke? In fact, what if they didn't even have a script? What if the director just said, "Okay, Bruce and Michelle, you are on the brink of divorce. Now, in your own words, reconcile. Action!" How ordinary would it feel? When we've been hurt in marriage, no one hands us a script. No one tells us to practice our lines. And no one starts playing sentimental music that motivates our emotions to make us want to dig deep.

Don't get me wrong. Marriage conferences, counseling sessions, and stirring speeches play a part. I know that many couples walk into a conference or a counseling appointment feeling as if they are down by three touchdowns. The meetings help motivate them to move beyond the plain hard facts of the scoreboard and get back in the game. For us men, an inspirational session can realign our hearts with our wives, recalibrate our minds to God's purpose and plan for marriage, and recommit our souls to persevere through the emotional ups and downs. But eventually we leave the conference hotel or the counselor's office and get back to brass tacks. In *The Story of Us*, after the background music fades away and the dinner at Chow Funs is over, then what?

For Jason and Kristy, after their marriage conference pep talk, they still have to get back in the game. They'll resume their busy schedules, still have to deal with the kids, and weather the risks of future business trips. Eventually, the jokes and sentimental stories from the conference will fade from memory. The binder with all their notes will find its way to a shelf in a seldom-trafficked room. Soon, performances won't match expectations. If Jason simply relies on the emotion of a stirring halftime speech, he'll eventually sink back into himself. He'll slide down to the end of the bench when he gets knocked down and the game gets tough again. Injuries in marriage don't happen in the locker room; they happen on the field.

Injuries Happen on the Field, Not in the Locker Room

If we've seen them, certain sports scenes never fade from the hard drive of our minds.

Like Lawrence Taylor's leg-snapping tackle of Joe Theismann.

Or Mike Tyson's bite from Evander Holyfield's ear. Or Dale Earnhardt's final-lap crash on turn four of the Daytona 500. Regardless of the sport, injuries are inevitable. You never know if they will snuff out a career, mangle a body part, or take a life, but you know they'll happen.

I remember speaking at a marriage conference and having Jen bite off my ear during a break. Not literally, of course, but that's what it felt like. Our communication wires got crossed. I injured her with my words and she ripped off a biting comment in response.

It's one thing to have a fight at a marriage conference; I'm sure that happens all the time. It's quite another thing to have a fight at a marriage conference when you and your wife are the *speakers*. So, naturally, I saw this little spat as a great opportunity to love my wife as Christ loves the church, beautify my bride, and play hurt.

I stewed. I stammered. Like a turtle, I retreated silently into my shell. I didn't want to come off the bench and resolve the conflict in a healthy way. No one started a rising crescendo of music to stir my soul to action. When I get injured, I crave *vindication* for my injury far more than I crave *victory* in my marriage. I don't want to fight for God's glory; I just want to fight.

The real test in marriage won't be in the "locker room" of a conference or a counseling session, or as you read this book. It will be out on the field, in the course of daily life, when your wife hurls an insult your way, when she stiff-arms your advances, or when you find a receipt for a hotel in Manhattan when she was supposed to be with her friends in Boston.

Ever notice what happens whenever an athlete is injured on the field of play? The commentators show the replay from every possible angle, until we're nauseated and they've rooted out the precise cause of the injury. The downed player is immediately encircled by a cadre of trainers, teammates, coaches, doctors, and even members of the opposing team.

What happens when a man gets injured in the field of marriage? Nothing. Nobody comes to the rescue. No one offers commentary on why you didn't deserve such treatment. Your buddies don't come rushing through the door, circle around you, carefully lift you up and say, "It will be all right, man. Don't worry, we'll get her on the next play." If it were a battlefield, you'd be left for dead. In those moments you can't go back to the conference to hear another locker-room pep talk. You're alone, injured on the field. What do you do?

It seems as if every injury in marriage also damages our eyes. We're blinded to our real attackers and our allies are obscured from view.

Lessons from the Tunnel

Slithering on all fours through a dark, narrow passageway that would give munchkins claustrophobia, I rethought my decision to descend to the third level of the tunnel complex in the Cu Chi region of Vietnam. About 25 miles northwest of Saigon sits a monument to the tenacity of the Viet Cong. My tour guide, a former tunnel fighter, looked at me, the lone American in the group, and said, "The U.S. never took the tunnels." Though he ambushed my national pride, it didn't take me long to see why. The American GIs were fighting an enemy committed to guerilla warfare; our strategists grossly underestimated the elaborate tunnel system; and our initial plan of attack involved dropping a reluctant volunteer into the dark abyss—by himself.

For years, the Viet Cong lived in the backyard of our largest and strongest American base, Saigon. Such close proximity produced an uneasy union, defined by months of peace interrupted by short bursts of conflict. American patrols moving through "cleared" areas in the Cu Chi region would be ambushed by unseen attackers.

Not realizing how deep and extensive the tunnel system was—by some reports, the tunnels stretched for 125 miles, on three levels—for years the Americans retaliated the same way: calling in the bombers, hurling grenades into tunnel openings, and dropping hesitant GIs into the dark passageways—alone. The Viet Cong retreated, but never for long. During the course of the war, the U.S. Army never rooted out the tunnel warriors, and the Viet Cong never gained any ground. The only perceivable result was casualties on both sides.

Many marriages are marked by months of peace interrupted by short bursts of conflict. It can feel as if you're fighting the same battles over the same ground. Every few months, you argue about the budget. You feel as if your wife is wasting money and you can't buy the things you want to have. She wounds you in public—again. Your in-laws can't appreciate how you've taken care of their daughter. The nightly headache alarm goes off about the same time as your passion bell. Your prayer life together consists of a hastily recited blessing at the dinner table.

When Jen wounds my ego, or I feel guilty about not leading spiritually, or my libido is starved, I tend to retaliate in the same ways: retreat quickly or hurl verbal grenades. Eventually, the dust settles and we discover a few more months of peace. But no ground is gained. The only result of this uneasy union is casualties on both sides. Playing hurt means that we take the time to identify the unseen attacker, become aware of the traps, and stop fighting repeated battles by reluctantly dropping into the dark abyss alone.

The Real Attacker: A Crafty Guerilla

General William Westmoreland, commander of military operations in Vietnam, made the claim, "We never lost a battle." But we didn't win the war. Though superior in manpower and firepower, we didn't have much experience fighting against guerilla tactics.

Guerilla means "little war." It describes a conflict between armed civilians and a regular army, in which the civilians use tactics such as ambush, sabotage, surprise, and extraordinary mobility to strike and withdraw almost immediately. Guerilla tactics change the battlefield, because the enemy never meets you head-on. He negates your strength by luring you into a place of unfamiliarity and discomfort. In Vietnam, where the Americans relied on military strength and superior firepower, the Viet Cong utilized their labyrinth of tunnels and the ability to blend into the population to exploit their mobility and the element of surprise to undermine the U.S. Army's strength.

Above ground, the American military's strength was matchless. Below ground, the Americans stepped on the Viet Cong's home turf—at a decided disadvantage.

The Vietnam War was far different from any other war the Americans had engaged. It was a series of minor skirmishes rather than major battles. But after a decade of minor skirmishes, the country with the greater munitions, manpower, and muscle lost heart and left the field. Ultimately, the Viet Cong recognized that the goal wasn't to defeat the Marines on the battlefield; it was to defeat hearts in Kansas. Time was on their side. If they could simply keep the fight going, eventually the Americans would quit and go home. Just as the French had a few years before.

The enemy we face in marriage isn't our wives. Instead, it's a crafty guerilla fighter, whose goal is not to defeat us in major battles, but simply to keep us engaged in minor skirmishes until we eventually lose heart and possibly leave home. The enemy's name means "adversary." You may know him by a different name: Satan.

I know; I just lost half my audience.

I'm not sure where you sit on the "Satan spectrum." Perhaps you see the devil behind every lost job and flat tire. He's everywhere. Or maybe you can't think of Satan without picturing one of Dana Carvey's Church Lady skits from *Saturday Night Live* (check it out on YouTube), in which Satan is nothing more than a caricature. Or you might be somewhere in the middle.

We tend to make two common mistakes when it comes to the person known as Satan: We either ascribe too much power to him or not enough. Most American men fall into the latter group. One of my favorite movie lines comes from Kevin Spacey's character in *The Usual Suspects*: "The greatest trick the devil ever pulled was convincing the world he didn't exist."

Unless your Bible is an NPV (New Perforated Version), which allows you to tear out sections that make you uncomfortable, you can't ignore the reality of an invisible adversary. In the same letter in which the apostle Paul gives us his playbook for marriage, he also rips back the curtain on the unseen world: "Be strong in the Lord and in the strength of his might. Put on the whole armor of God, that you may be able to stand *against the schemes of the devil*. For we do not wrestle against flesh and blood, but against the rulers, against the authorities, against the cosmic powers over this present darkness, *against the spiritual forces of evil in the heavenly places*" (Ephesians 6:10–12, emphasis added). Cue the eerie music.

We learn a couple things from Paul's statements in Ephesians. (For the full context, see Ephesians 5:22–6:9.) First, when it comes to conflict in our interpersonal relationships (husbands and wives, children and parents, employers and employees), we aren't battling against flesh and blood. Although we might feel attacked by our wives or our children or our bosses, the real enemy is the unseen "accuser" (see Revelation 12:10) who wants to exploit the division and destroy our most important relationships. That doesn't mean we can abdicate our personal responsibility in the conflict. (After I give Jen the silent treatment I can't say, "It wasn't my fault. Satan shut my lips.") But it means far more is at stake than simply getting justice for our injuries.

Though Satan and his minions remain invisible to the naked eye, their schemes are fairly predictable. As Paul says, "We are not ignorant of his schemes" (2 Corinthians 2:11 NASB). Satan doesn't have to cause conflict between husbands and wives— that happens naturally enough—but he's quick to sniff blood in the water. As Peter says, "Be of sober spirit, be on the alert. Your adversary, the devil, prowls around like a roaring lion, seeking someone to devour" (1 Peter 5:8 NASB). Like guerilla fighters, demons mobilize quickly to exploit a weakness. Satan didn't force Eve to eat from the forbidden tree; but he was quick to drop some justifying phrases into her mind when she saw the fruit glimmering in the morning sun. He didn't make Jen bite off my ear at the conference; but after I was hurt, the devil, or one of his lackeys, could have easily been whispering in my ear, setting traps:

"You don't deserve to be treated like that."
"What gives her the right to demand her way?"
"It's about time you stand up for yourself."

Even though Satan's name means *adversary*, his adversary is not God. They are not counterbalanced forces in the universe. Though Satan tempted God—in the person of Jesus Christ in the wilderness—he cannot lift a finger against humanity without God's permission (see Job 1–2; Luke 22:31). The devil reminds me of a dog on one of those retractable leashes. At any moment, God can yank back the chain. For reasons that will ultimately bring God glory, Satan is allowed a long leash on earth. And because Satan cannot attack his master, he wants to bite and devour what's most precious to God instead.

Let's say you're an assassin assigned to kill a famous artist, who is surrounded by bodyguards and a security system. After scouting out his home, you realize the defenses are impenetrable. You can't touch him. What's your next plan of attack? If you can't destroy the artist, you can hurt him by damaging his works of art. So you set your sights on destroying, marring, and scarring his greatest creations. That's Satan. He knows his limitations. When Paul refers to the devil's "schemes" in Ephesians 6:11, the word connotes "lying in wait." He's like a teenage tagger who waits in the shadows for the cars to pass before he whips out his spray paint. Satan lurks and prowls, waiting for a chance to vandalize God's living portraits whenever the defenses come down.

Maybe you're thinking, *Come on, Brian. Satan's not wasting his time on me. My marriage is just one of countless others.* Let me tell you something: If you said, "I do," God is using your marriage to paint a work of art to display his glory to the world. If Satan can exploit your conflict to destroy or dampen your love for your wife, it's as if he just sprayed graffiti all over another one of God's masterpieces.

Take some time this week to read through the book of Genesis, and notice how many family squabbles take center stage. Abraham lies about Sarah multiple times. Isaac and Rebekah show differing favoritism to Jacob and Esau. Jacob benefits from the childbearing rivalry between Leah and Rachel. Though each individual is culpable for his or her actions, one can be certain that Satan somehow slithered onto the scene.

Since he cannot scare the Creator, he sets out to scar the creation. And he's doing a decent job. His MO hasn't changed since Adam and Eve blamed everyone but themselves for the apple turnovers they ate thousands of years ago. Ever since, Satan has tried to ram a wedge between husbands and wives by convincing them the bull's-eye for their anger, pain, and vindication belongs on their spouse.

Vietnam was such a difficult place to fight because the American soldiers could not distinguish friend from foe. The Viet Cong looked exactly like South Vietnamese villagers. Once you've been wounded enough by people you thought were on your side, you stop believing the best about them. You live on edge.

When I start questioning whether Jen is my friend or foe, I'm on edge. I'm anxious. And I can believe the worst about her. The last thing I want to do is play hurt for someone who I believe is embarrassing me in public, or starving my libido, or hasn't encouraged me in a while. I won't sacrifice much for someone I believe might be my enemy. When I forget there's a guerilla fighter lurking about to exploit my injuries, I'm willing to align myself more with the real attacker than the ally that God gave me for life—my wife. I'm willing to hear the devil's accusations about her. I entertain his whispers about why her infractions justify my retaliation.

Paul refocuses our gunsights: Stand *against the schemes of the devil. For we do not wrestle against flesh and blood.* Next time you're in a squabble, fight, or moment of "intense fellowship," notice the red in your wife's cheeks. That blood rushing to her skin reminds you that, no matter how much you might want to see her as your enemy, she's not. Insert your wife's name in the following sentence, then say it out loud: "_____ is not my enemy."

For oneness to work in your marriage, you will need to *crave victory* in building your relationship with your wife far more than you *crave vindication* for your injuries. One of my mentors, who interviewed hundreds of couples on what makes a successful marriage, said, "The number one hallmark of great marriages are spouses who are more aware of the damage done to their mate than the damage done to themselves."[1]

As long as Satan keeps us engaged in minor skirmishes, we begin to lose heart for our marriages. Furthermore, the devil will have won on two fronts. If we have a problem with our wives, we will also have a problem with our heavenly Father. Peter tells husbands that our prayers will be hindered if we're at odds with our wives. We may cry "Abba," but he won't answer if we're not cherishing our brides. In other words, we lose our "air support." When we choose to retaliate against our wives, our unseen enemy rejoices that we are moving away from our brides *and* our God. We can't love God and hate his daughters.

When I've been hurt in my marriage, the last person I think of is Satan or some unseen attacker. I either retreat from the conflict to lick my wounds, or I immediately go after the one who wounded me, namely Jen. Either way, when I set out on a course of vindication rather than victory, I descend into the tunnels of my mind. Like an untrained American soldier at Cu Chi, I leave behind my "air support" and step down into enemy territory. On edge, anxious, and hot under the collar, I walk right into four carefully placed traps: persuasion, punishment, pity, and performance.

The Traps

The Viet Cong became experts in American fighting tactics. They spent years scheming ways to lure, entrap, and kill American soldiers. For example, they knew that our soldiers had been trained to jump into a corner for maximum cover when entering a room. So, in the tunnels, where they had rooms for everything from hospitals to barracks, the Viet Cong constructed fake floors in the corners, covering punji stakes laced with poison or human excrement.

When a column of unsuspecting Marines walked into an ambush, the Viet Cong fired off a few shots before retreating into the complex tunnel system. They knew if the Americans wanted retribution, they would have to come underground and face the Viet Cong on their own turf. With each small step in the darkness, the young Marine scouts would inch ever closer to a carefully constructed trap. In war, retribution is fatal, but necessary. In marriage, it's only fatal.

At that marriage conference, when Jen snapped at me, I craved retribution. I failed to recognize that my battle was not against flesh and blood, and instead saw her as my primary attacker. Anxious for vindication, I descended to the enemy's turf and began inching my way in the darkness toward four traps. First, I wanted Jen to be *persuaded* of her irrational thoughts. Second, I wanted Jen to be *punished* for her insensitivity. Third, I wanted Jen to *pity* me in my injured state. And finally, I started thinking Jen should *perform* differently. Inflammatory phrases started jumping to mind: "She ought to be more understanding. She's so quick to jump on my back. She'll probably never change."

Rather than attack the problem, I attacked the person. I could have silenced the thoughts that were firing like machine guns in my mind; I could have assumed the best about my wife and worked toward victory in our marriage. Instead, I jumped down into the tunnels.

I started logically walking through the argument so I could *persuade* Jen why her words were far more hurtful than what I had said. After she lobbed her verbal grenade, I emotionally *punished* her with silence. I pushed my pain deep down, like an array of punji sticks ready to be tripped over in the next few days or weeks. Rather than engage Jen in conversation and explain why her words had hurt me, I found my way to my solitary foxhole to brood until I gained her *pity*. Once the wedge between us had been set, it was easy to make mental notes of every time she blew it. From there I could start comparing Jen's perceived weaknesses with the imagined strengths of other women. And before long I would be back to demanding that Jen *perform* (look, say, do) to earn my love and sacrifice. Only when she started measuring up would I move toward her again.

As men, when we're injured on the field of marriage, we instinctively want payback. Maybe you fall into one trap more than another. Maybe you punish with verbal grenades rather than emotional land mines. Maybe you argue your case like a well-trained lawyer. Maybe you avoid the pain because you're afraid of confrontation. Or you opt for the pity play until your wife caves in and takes responsibility for the outburst. Maybe each altercation pushes you into the trap of wishing your wife performed differently than she does. But with each snare, you drive the wedge deeper into your relationship.

Peter, one of the disciples who we know was married, strikes me as a guy quick to pay back through punishment. When a guard tried to handcuff Jesus in the garden of Gethsemane, Peter stole a sword and sliced off the man's ear. Jesus rebuked him. Something must have sunk in, because after Jesus' resurrection, Peter changed his fighting tactics. In the same letter in which he warns husbands to treasure God's daughters, he writes, "To sum up, all of you be harmonious, sympathetic, brotherly, kindhearted, and humble in spirit; not returning evil for evil or insult for insult, but giving a blessing instead; for you were called for the very purpose that you might inherit a blessing" (1 Peter 3:8–9 NASB). In other words, if we want to experience something other than casualties in our marriages, we'll have to change our fighting tactics. God doesn't promise an injury-free life. On the contrary, Peter says we must be ready to endure insults, evil, and pain in our relationships. We will continue to fall into the same traps of persuasion, punishment, pity, and performance if we return insult for insult. Instead of payback, we need to push through the pain and play hurt.

GAME FILM

Scripture highlights emotional pain, rather than hiding it. The men and women we perceive as heroes in the Bible have just as many great foibles as great feats of faith. When you read the letters of Paul, you see a man quite frustrated with his relationships. One could say that Paul had a bride in every port. They weren't named Kristy, Sally, or Jen, but Ephesus, Galatia, and Corinth. Unlike me when I'm hurt by something Jen has said or done, Paul didn't bury his frustrations. When injured by one of the churches he founded,

Paul didn't pay them back through persuasion, punishment, pity, or performance. Instead, he loved them enough to tackle the problem without attacking the people. His goal was victory rather than vindication.

One of Paul's problem "brides" was the church he'd helped to plant in the port town of Corinth, the Las Vegas of Macedonia. Though Paul wrote often to Corinth, we have only two of his letters preserved in Scripture. He got stung by plenty of darts from this young church: he heard they preferred other preachers to him (1 Corinthians 3); they slept around with others inside and outside the church (1 Corinthians 5); they made others feel like second-class Christians if they didn't exhibit the right gifts of the Spirit (1 Corinthians 12–14); and they debated whether Paul had the right credentials to lead them (2 Corinthians 11:5–6; 12:11–13).

Now, because Paul compares loving a wife to loving a church, let's pretend those same complaints were from a marriage. As husbands, how should we respond? Here's a wife who constantly compares her husband's abilities to other men's, she sleeps around, she treats him like a second-class citizen because he doesn't appear as spiritual as she is, and she wonders whether or not he has the ability to lead their family. Chances are, you've felt wounded by some of those experiences. Listen to how Paul deals with the pain from those wounds:

> I wrote to you out of *much affliction and anguish of heart and with many tears,* not to cause you pain but to let you know the abundant love that I have for you. Now if anyone has caused pain, he has caused it not to me, but in some measure—not to put it too severely—to all of you. For such a one, this punishment by the majority is enough, so you should rather turn to forgive and comfort him, or he may be overwhelmed by excessive sorrow. So I beg you to reaffirm your love for him. For this is why I wrote, that I might test you and know whether you are obedient in everything. *Anyone whom you forgive, I also forgive.* Indeed, what I have forgiven, if I have forgiven anything, has been for your sake in the presence of Christ, *so that we*

would not be outwitted by Satan; for we are not ignorant of his designs. (2 Corinthians 2:4–11, emphasis added)

For the *love of Christ controls us*, because we have concluded this: that one has died for all, therefore all have died. (2 Corinthians 5:14, emphasis added)

Here for the *third time* I am ready to come to you. And I will not be a burden, for I seek not what is yours but you. . . . I will most *gladly spend and be spent for your souls*. If I love you more, am I to be loved less? (2 Corinthians 12:14–15, emphasis added)

Notice several points of importance for our marriages:

1. Paul doesn't deny the pain from his "spouse," but doesn't return insult for insult.
2. Paul recognizes the enemy's role in wanting to exploit the confrontation.
3. Paul is compelled more by the love of Christ than the pain from his wounds. In other words, he strives to "be like Christ" even when he doesn't feel like it.
4. Paul pursues the ones who pained him (for the third time he's trying to connect with them).

Rather than fall prey to traps in the tunnels of his mind, Paul played hurt. Rather than pursue vindication, he pursued victory. Does this mean Paul was a doormat? No, he was quick to point out the pain inflicted upon him from people in the church; but he never allowed his pain to dominate his thinking. He valued oneness with the church more than justice for his wounds. Though the church created countless problems for Paul, he refused to believe they were the problem.

When I have problems with my marriage, I inevitably think that Jen's the problem. Paul pushes through that lie. When wounded, I retreat. Paul advances. When pained, I punish. Paul pursues. When insulted, I insult. Paul forgives. We'll discover in chapter 7 how men who love like Christ loves will advance when they want to retreat and play hurt when they want to pay back.

No one said that playing hurt would be easy or even fair. Whether we knew it or not, when we got married, we didn't sign up for equal rights, but the right to die to ourselves. We signed up to love like Christ loves. We signed up to beautify our brides. We signed up to take the hits and turn the other cheek.

Does that sound more like the job of an apostle—with a capital A? Peter and Paul never claimed to be "super apostles." In fact, quite the contrary. Paul called himself the least of all apostles and the chief of all sinners. Neither apostle claimed credit for being able to play hurt and love like Christ loved. No natural ability or past success enabled them to take on such an assignment. They knew that to love supernaturally took more than their own natural power. It required something most men run away from: dependence on others.

Dropping in Alone

As I crawled on all fours through the tunnels of Cu Chi, and worried that my Vietnamese host would find a way to "lose" me in the maze, I realized that much had changed in the three decades since the end of the war. They had widened the tunnels for big Westerners like me. They had installed tiny lights to provide some illumination. And something else had changed . . . oh yeah, there were no hidden punji sticks, or trip wires attached to booby traps, or Viet Cong soldiers sitting in blind corners holding AK-47s! I shuddered to think about a lone American soldier, armed with nothing more than a pistol and a flashlight, crawling through these tunnels. In the same way, I see husbands all the time who think they can battle a cunning enemy without backup.

I had another counseling appointment with Jason and Kristy about three days after they returned from the marriage conference. They walked in like newlyweds—holding hands, swapping smiles, even a bit flirtatious. The "halftime speech" at the marriage conference had convinced them to move beyond payback and pursue victory in their marriage. Jason recognized that the real enemy in his marriage wasn't Kristy. He pinpointed how susceptible he was to the pity and performance traps.

It's amazing what a conference or counseling can do for a couple—and what it can't. I haven't seen Jason in about three months. After three visits and a weekend conference, he seemed to feel as if he was on the right path. I hope so. But my experience with husbands tells me that the enemy can use success in marriage just as much as he uses failure. He lures men into complacency, believing they've "cleared the area," until a few months—or even years—later, when they walk into another ambush. Their wives respond in an unexpected way. They feel the sting of disrespect. They start fighting major skirmishes over minor issues. Or they find their passions growing for pornography or the advances of a woman in the office. Whatever the surprise, they tend to fight those battles like they always had in the past. They drop in alone. But, whether he realizes it or not, every man has backup.

THE HOT SEAT

1. What ground do you keep fighting over in your marriage?

2. Have you ever thought of Satan as an enemy in your marriage? Why or why not?

3. When wounded in marriage, men tend to fall into one or more of these traps: *persuasion, punishment, pity,* or *performance.* Which ones tend to trip you up?

4. What do these traps look like in your marriage?

5. When you fall into one of those traps, do you tend to handle the fight alone? If not, who helps you walk through the battles?

Chapter 5

Allies Every Husband Needs

"IT'S JUST A FLESH WOUND! . . . Come back here. . . . I'll bite your legs off!"

It's too bad we can't put food on the table by watching Monty Python sketches all day. In this classic from *The Search for the Holy Grail*, the Black Knight blocks a creek crossing from Arthur, king of the Britons. Arthur tries enticing the knight to join his quest, but to no avail.

"No man shall pass!" replies the masked crusader. Arthur draws his sword and rushes his adversary. After a few, brief parries, Arthur, clearly the better swordsman, slices off one of the Black Knight's arms.

The king says, "Now, stand aside."

"'Tis but a scratch," protests the knight, and he proceeds to attack.

Arthur cuts off his other arm, "Victory is mine!"

The Black Knight starts kicking the king, "It's just a flesh wound."

Incredulous, the king says, "What are you going to do, bleed on me?"

"I'm invincible. The Black Knight always triumphs."

Finally, after Arthur dispatches the knight's legs, the king and his attendant clop across the creek. The stumpy knight yells back, "Running off are we? Come back here and take what's coming to you. I'll bite your legs off."

When I'm hurt in my marriage, I'm that guy blocking the bridge. Though I'm bleeding out all over the ground, I insist in my mind, "It doesn't hurt. It's just a flesh wound." But playing through pain is not the same thing as ignoring pain.

When a 330-pound offensive lineman writhes on the field, nobody yells out, "Get up, you big pansy! It's just a flesh wound!" When an athlete is injured on the field, everyone knows if he's in pain. When a man is injured on the field of marriage, often no one knows. When a linebacker shatters a quarterback's leg, the injured player doesn't think twice about leaning on teammates, trainers, and coaches for support. When a wife shatters her husband's ego, he typically doesn't lean on anyone. He simply looks at his wound, gushing with blood, and then responds, "'Tis but a scratch."

Every man I know hides his emotional wounds. Men are highly trained in the art of masking pain. Think about the first real wound in your life. I'm going to bet it's locked deep in the cellar of your heart, and few, if any, have gone down there with you.

When Bob was eight, he went to a lower-income elementary school that couldn't afford books for every student. He was paired up with another boy. Every time his schoolmate got to the end of a page, he looked at Bob with eyes wondering, *You done yet?* Not wanting to admit that he read at a glacial pace, Bob just nodded. Though he's now well over the hill, for most of his adult life Bob felt those same eyes and heard the same unspoken question from coworkers, bosses, teammates, and his wife: "You done yet? Are you ever going to catch up?"

Another friend of mine, whom I've known for six years, recently confided in me that his dad had hit him when he was thirteen. Another friend was sexually abused by a cousin when he was five. Another man who has gone to church his whole life has always felt as if, no matter how much good he does, God still expects him to do better. These men are strong, successful, and stealthy. Over time, men learn how to mask their pain.

For years, I never shared my battle with jealousy, insecurity and comparison. Then I heard an older man, very successful in his field, who was honest enough to say, "I've come to realize I'm insecure. No, I'm desperately insecure." It was the first time I'd heard a man say *ouch*.

Ever since the garden of Eden, men have mastered the art of covering their shame and pain with fig leaves. The same is true in marriage. Rather than cry for help, we run for cover. I'm not suggesting we walk around flashing bracelets etched with our ailments: "Doubts Self-Worth," or "Addicted to Porn," or "Physically Abused." But somehow we need to start airing out our wounds. Every fifteen-year-old in a first-aid class will tell you that unless you clean the wound, you never heal. As I said in the previous chapter, every injury in marriage affects a man's eyesight. He's blinded to his real adversary and his allies fade from view. God has given every man a couple of medics ready to rush to his side if he would just cry out: men in his life that are within earshot.

Some wounds require expert surgeons, but I think the bulk of the wounds inflicted on men can and should be treated in the company of other men. When a man goes down on the football field or the battlefield, other men rush to his aid. But when a man develops the habit of hiding his emotional wounds, no one knows when he's down. That's one reason I like being around guys in recovery. Whether it's alcoholics or sex addicts, they've learned through their own brokenness the need to cry, "Medic!" Just as a scratch can eventually turn into gangrene, minor emotional cuts can turn into major infections. Many marriages are ruined on nothing more than years of festering bitterness caused by minor irritations over things long forgotten. Instead of saying "ouch," we stubbornly proclaim, "Nah, it's just a flesh wound. I'm fine."

Teammates

What's the craziest thing you've ever done? Write it down in the margin. I bet it was dangerous. There's a good chance it involved the police. And I'd wager my son's college education it involved other guys. Chances are, someone acted as your accomplice or as your audience. Living in Charlotte, home of NASCAR, where people spend five hours watching left-hand turns, I've heard a few redneck jokes—like this one: What are a redneck's famous last words?

"Guys, hold my beer and watch this."

Men do crazy things when other men are around. But they also achieve the impossible. First guys to conquer Mount Everest: Tenzing Norgay and Sir Edmund Hillary. First Americans to find a passage from the Mississippi to the Northwest: Meriwether Lewis and William Clark. First guys to fly a plane: Wilbur and Orville Wright. First guys to land on the moon: Neil Armstrong and Buzz Aldrin. What's the common element between all those firsts?

The word *and*. Crazy only requires spectators. But great missions, whether conquering a mountain or the moon, requires camaraderie. When you open the New Testament, you discover men (plural) on a mission. Even Jesus didn't venture out alone.

First thing he did after he started his public ministry? Surrounded himself with other guys (Mark 1:16–20). First time Jesus sent out the disciples? They went out like Noah's animals— two by two (see Mark 6:7–13). When the first churches were established, they were founded by pairs of men: Peter and John (Acts 3–5); Barnabas and Saul (Acts 13–15); Paul and Silas (Acts 16–18). *And* is a powerful word.

Who follows the *and* in your life? Who are your "and" guys? Walk through the letters of Paul and you'll discover he never went anywhere without some trusted companions:

Timothy, my fellow worker, greets you; so do Lucius and Jason and Sosipater . . . (Romans 16:21)

Paul . . . and our brother Sosthenes, to the church of God that is in Corinth . . . (1 Corinthians 1:1–2)

I rejoice at the coming of Stephanas and Fortunatus and Achaicus . . . for they refreshed my spirit. (1 Corinthians 16:17–18)

Paul . . . and Timothy our brother . . . (2 Corinthians 1:1)

Paul . . . and all the brothers who are with me . . . (Galatians 1:1–2)

So that you also may know how I am and what I am doing, Tychicus the beloved brother and faithful minister in the Lord will tell you everything. (Ephesians 6:21)

Paul and Timothy . . . to all the saints in Christ Jesus who are at Philippi. (Philippians 1:1; see also Colossians 1:1)

Aristarchus my fellow prisoner greets you, and Mark . . . and Jesus who is called Justus. . . . Ephaphras, who is one of you . . . greets you. . . . Luke the beloved physician greets you, as does Demas. (Colossians 4:10–14)

Paul, Silvanus, and Timothy, to the church of the Thessalonians . . . (1 Thessalonians 1:1; 2 Thessalonians 1:1)

When I send Artemas or Tychicus to you, do your best to come to me at Nicopolis, for I have decided to spend the winter there. (Titus 3:12)

In all but one of his thirteen letters, Paul mentions men who are in his foxhole with him. The only exception is 1 Timothy, which is addressed to one of Paul's most trusted "and" guys (see Philippians 2:19–22).

Crack open your Bible and find 2 Timothy 4:9–22. Here we have Paul's last known written words. Last words can reveal a person's heart. How do Paul's last words strike you? Twice he appeals to Timothy: "Do your best to come to me soon. . . . Do your best to come before winter" (4:9, 21). He laments losing some "and" guys to ministry (Crescens, Titus, and Tychicus), and others to betrayal (Demas, Alexander). You can feel distress flow from his pen: "Luke alone is with me" (4:11). When Paul speaks of these men, it's because he had come to rely on them. He needed them. They weren't just spectators for some crazy antics.

Quick, think about your wedding pictures. Specifically imagine the one with your groomsmen. Maybe you were sporting blue ruffled tuxedo shirts. Maybe you had one guy beside you. Maybe you had ten. If you retook the picture today, how many of those guys would still be standing beside you? And how many would really know what's going on in your life? Granted, we live in a mobile and transient culture, so chances may be slim that you still live near your groomsmen. Even so, could you fill their spots with other men who you would say are "and" guys? We invite other men to stand with us at the wedding, but rarely to stand beside us throughout the marriage.

As men, we tend to fall into the trap of thinking that we conquered Mount Everest on our wedding day. In reality, we just hit base camp. Painting a living portrait of God's glory by loving our wives sacrificially for fifty years is Mount Everest. Can you imagine Sir Edmund Hilary reaching base camp in the Himalayas and saying to his Sherpa guide, Tenzing Norgay, "Hey, I got it from here—later." Yet we leave most of our "and" guys at the altar and head up the mountain of marriage solo.

GAME FILM

Solomon, a man who puts dunce caps on Mensa members, wrote, "Whoever isolates himself seeks his own desire; he breaks out against all sound judgment" (Proverbs 18:1). Solomon ought to know. He blew the wisdom lottery ticket. Early in Solomon's life, God granted him one wish. Already guaranteed King David's inheritance, Solomon asked for wisdom. God granted his wish; yet Solomon, who was sought after for his acumen by kings and queens, squandered wisdom in his own life. When we read his personal journal (the book of Ecclesiastes), we see a man who abandoned sound wisdom to chase selfish desires. In the end, his pursuits of hedonism, intellectualism, and materialism led him to meaninglessness. I can't prove it, but somehow I think Ecclesiastes 12:1–8 describes Solomon in his last days, as a strong man bent over whose "grinders cease because they are few, and those who look through the windows [eyes] are dimmed" (12:3). Rocking back and forth on his front porch, he reflects on his hedonistic marathon run: "Remember also your Creator in the days of your youth. . . . Fear God and keep his commandments, for this is the whole duty of man. For God will bring every deed into judgment, with every secret thing, whether good or evil" (12:1, 13–14). So the man who traded divine wisdom for human existentialism proved he wasn't smarter than a fifth grader. Any child raised in Sunday school could reveal Solomon's wisdom that he gained after chasing foolishness: fear God and follow him.

Elsewhere in Scripture, Solomon writes poetry espousing the joys of loving one woman for a lifetime. His steamy Song of Songs relives his passion for a peasant woman (more than likely his first wife). In Proverbs 5:18, Solomon instructs husbands to "rejoice in the wife of your youth." And in Ecclesiastes, he concludes, "Enjoy life with the wife whom you love, all the days of your vain [brief] life" (9:9). After having 300 wives and 700 concubines, Solomon concluded it was far easier to love the woman you have than long for the woman you don't. The perfect spouse is the present spouse.

It's no surprise we don't see any "and" guys in Solomon's life. When we look at the tragic figures in Scripture, we notice how hard it is to fill in the blank after the *and*:

- Samson and _____ (someone other than Delilah).
- King Saul and _____
- After he sent all his "and" guys away to battle and decided to grab some rays on the roof, King David and _____ (someone other than Bathsheba)
- Jonah and _____
- Judas Iscariot and _____
- Solomon and _____

The blank shouts a warning to us across the centuries: "Whoever isolates himself . . . breaks out against all sound judgment" (Proverbs 18:1).

God didn't design us to drop in the tunnels alone. "And" guys rebuke, refocus, recharge, and remind us that the goal of marriage is not our personal happiness. They rebuke us when we crave the immediate over the eternal. They help us refocus on the mission of marriage: God's glory—his fame and his name. They remind us that our adversary doesn't share our address.

Men identify quickly with other guys in most every other context besides marriage. Growing up in the neighborhood, boys form a club. Without guidance, boys join a gang. Guys talk about their "boyz," "entourage," and "crew." Beer commercials highlight a guy's "wingman." So how do you find "and" guys for your marriage mission?

Seek them out. Isolated men seek out their own destruction. Wise men seek out trusted companions. Chances are, you've got guys who share your affinities for sports, business, or hobbies. *Spend regular time with them.* Grab a coffee before work. Go on a camping trip. Get a regular time on the calendar. I've learned that if I don't schedule it, it won't happen. I can make buddies accidentally, but developing "and" guys requires intentionality. This last part might be the most difficult: *share your scars.*

Men love to share past pains. Get guys in a room and eventually you'll hear stories about their injuries. My brother-in-law's legs look like someone beat him with a metal chain. Each divot and jagged scar tells a story about some mountain or road bike accident. "I got this one when a car turned into me. Oh, you should have seen this crash. When my knee skidded on that stump, it felt like someone cut me open with a chain saw."

When men get real with the rawness in their lives, they invite others to share their wounds. They realize they aren't alone. But in order to find teammates, someone has to step up and pull back the curtain. Be brave. Share your scars first.

Right now you're thinking, *Brian, I can hear my wife say, "Oh, yeah, so the book tells you to have another guys' night out!"* The reason your wife doesn't like guys' night out is because you go to a bar and talk sports with your buddies. Nothing wrong with that every now and again, but "and" guys get together and talk about scars. Here's a quick comparison between buddies and "and" guys:

Buddies	"And" Guys
Get together and watch sports	Get together and share scars
Encourage you to wife bash	Encourage you to beautify your wife
Say you deserve better	Encourage you to sacrifice
Magnify your wife's weaknesses	Magnify your wife's strengths
Help you crave vindication for wounds	Help you crave victory despite your wounds
Gawk at other women	Guard your eyes against other women

Find some "and" guys in your life and your wife will help you schedule the next guys' night out.

Cairns and Coaches

Mount Oberlin juts into the Montana sky like a rocky sail over Glacier National Park. A few years back, I climbed the 8,000-foot peak with my father-in-law. When I told him I had grown up hiking mountains in the East, he chuckled. We set off on a well-worn dirt path, through fields of wildflowers, over streams, and up the side of the mountain. Along the way, we talked to a few mountain goats. As the scrub pines slimmed out, I gazed up at the ascent. Above the tree line, where the path ended, I discovered how the Rocky Mountains got their name. Now with nothing to shield us from the sun, we ascended the scree field, a wide swath of broken up bits of rock and shale that cover the shoulders of the peaks in the Rockies.

You won't find scree fields in the East, but they are an orthopedic surgeon's dream. For every step forward, I could easily slide back two. My ankles issued a notice: "We strenuously object to the proposed path." As I looked upslope, I couldn't tell which way to go. The shale shifted like snake skin.

The time leading up to the wedding day feels like the first few miles of hiking Mount Oberlin. Well-worn dirt paths. Wildflowers. A few friendly goats. Nothing too demanding. More like a stroll than a strenuous hike. But you don't have to be married for very long before you encounter the scree fields of sexual frustration, communication conundrums, and debilitating disputes. For every step forward, you can slide back two. In a scree field, it can feel as if you're constantly covering the same ground.

As I slogged through the scree, turning both ankles and feeling Bunsen burners light up my calves, my father-in-law encouraged me to pick up the pace by saying, "You know, just last month your mother-in-law made it up this mountain." After that dig, he pointed out mounds of shale that had been stacked up into cairns. They dotted the landscape like stone flags. Cairns are markers that indicate two things: you're on the right path, and you're not the only one to hike this mountain. Cairns act like silent coaches. They urge you up the mountain, giving you short-term goals to shoot for. It's still your effort, but the cairns make the task seem possible as they keep you on the right path.

Have you noticed that men will seek counsel in almost every arena except marriage? I don't know your profession, but imagine the best person in your field. How much would you be willing to pay for a lunch with such an expert? A hundred dollars? Two hundred? How about $2.63 million? Every year since 2000, a lunch with billionaire investor and philanthropist Warren Buffett has been auctioned off on eBay, to raise money for a nonprofit foundation in San Francisco. The highest bidder (and seven friends) receives three hours with the investment guru at a New York steak house—and the tab. The money goes to charity, but the wisdom goes to the highest bidder.

What do you suppose they talked about at that lunch? I doubt the eight winners came to the table asking Warren Buffett who was on his fantasy football team. I bet they didn't say, "So, what do you want to talk about?" No doubt they had a notepad full of investment questions, and more than likely they didn't get past the first three.

When we get together as men, we need to talk about things that matter. We aren't the only ones to hike the mountain of marriage, and yet it seems as if we spend a great deal of time scampering by ourselves through the scree fields with no real direction, encouragement, or support. There are cairns all around us, but like most men, we don't have the courage to stop and ask directions. We want to blaze our own trail through the slippery shale. It may cost $2.63 million to bend Warren Buffet's ear, but it only takes about $25 to find an expert marriage coach. The best money I ever spent was taking an older couple out to lunch to hear how they navigated the tough climbs in marriage. Anybody can walk through wildflowers on well-worn paths; few know how to get to the summits above the scree fields. So when you come across the cairns of a thriving marriage, move toward them.

On the scree field of conflict resolution, I learned that great marriages happen when spouses are more aware of the damage done to their mate than the damage done to themselves. On the mountain of raising kids, I picked up that there isn't just one sex talk, there's a series. When it comes to communicating to my wife, I was taught a simple question to ask her: "Are you asking for my ear or my brain?" On the slippery slope of romance, a wise older friend told me, "Treat your wife like you would treat your best client." On the scree field of sex, I learned, "Meet her needs first and you won't need to worry about your own."

What scree field are you on right now? Somewhere nearby is a cairn couple who has been up that mountain. They don't have a perfect marriage, but you can tell they're more than roommates. Get out your smartphone and enter these questions for your next lunch:

- → What are your best practices?
- → What would you do differently if you could?
- → What have been your greatest challenges? How did you get through them?
- → What do you wish someone would have told you when you were starting your marriage?
- → What keeps the fire burning in the bedroom as you add decades to your marriage?
- → How did you learn to handle conflict?

Every year you probably get a physical. You take your car in for regular maintenance. We maintain what is valuable. What about your marriage? I met one couple that starts their yearly vacation with a marriage conference. They call it their yearly tune-up. It helps them reflect, refocus, recharge, and remind themselves of why their marriage is anything but ordinary. Whether it's a weekend getaway to "get it together"[1] or picking up the check at lunch for a "cairn couple," you'll be surprised how such a small investment can pay huge dividends.

Most guys who play through pain have a coach urging them on. I've learned that men in the twilight of their lives want to have a great impact, but they don't believe the younger generation cares about what they say. As you traverse the well-worn paths of Scripture, you'll notice "and" passages, which depict older men building into the younger generation: Jethro helping Moses with an organizational chart; Barnabas rebuilding John Mark's self-esteem; Eli training Samuel through seminary; Paul teaching Titus how to pastor: "Older men are to be sober minded, dignified, self-controlled, sound in faith, in love, and in steadfastness. . . . Urge the younger men to be self-controlled" (Titus 2:2, 6).

In the Pastoral Epistles, Paul models the kind of coaching he wants in the DNA of the church. Older men have climbed the mountains that younger men want to conquer. Their character stands as cairns for the next generation. God knows that older men desire to leave a legacy, and that younger men want to build one. "Isolated men break out against all sound judgment." Going your marriage alone is like trying to hike the Rocky Mountains while ignoring the cairns.

Is it time to schedule a lunch?

I remember the first time I trained for a sprint triathlon. I'd never done any kind of competitive swimming, so I just started by doing some laps. After working my way up to about ten laps without needing a snorkel, I started gaining confidence. During one training session, I noticed the high school coach evaluating my stroke. Being a typical guy, I started swimming faster, hoping to impress him. I must have thought he might ask if I had any eligibility left. When I got out of the pool, I asked him for some pointers. He said, "You're trying way too hard. You're working against the water. If you would just dip your shoulders like a pendulum, the water would glide right by your body."

That one tip took minutes off my time and made swimming far more enjoyable. I'm sure if I had worked with him for a few sessions he would've improved my stroke immeasurably.

It's too bad there's such a negative stigma about marriage counseling. Most guys feel "dragged" into the therapist's office. In reality, trained counselors are like coaches. They watch what you're doing and how you're interacting as a couple, and see what you don't see. Most of us are expending huge amounts of energy in ways that work against our marriage. But from our vantage point, we're blinded. Counseling won't lessen the effort that marriage requires, but it can make the swim far more enjoyable. If you're dealing with deep-rooted issues or a problem you can't seem to solve, it's well worth the money to talk to a trained coach. When you think about a marriage counselor, just replace "counselor" with "coach" and be willing to ask for some pointers.

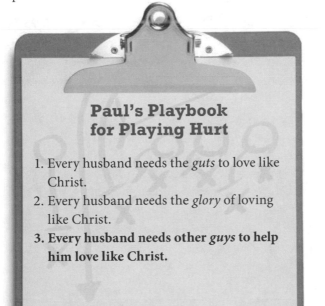

Paul's Playbook for Playing Hurt

1. Every husband needs the *guts* to love like Christ.
2. Every husband needs the *glory* of loving like Christ.
3. **Every husband needs other *guys* to help him love like Christ.**

THE HOT SEAT

1. Who are some "and" guys in your life? Have you had many in your past? What do you do to maintain those relationships?

2. What are some wounds that created scars in your life? Any with your dad? Any with your wife? With whom can you share those scars?

3. Who could be a "cairn couple" that you walk by each week? What would it take for you to spend some time with them?

4. Write down three questions you'd love to ask that couple. Be a man and pick up the tab.

Chapter 6

A Husband's Nutritional Guide

Do you have one of those "Real Men Love Jesus" bumper stickers? Take off the "love Jesus" part. (Don't worry, you won't get struck by lightning.) Now, fill in the blank with some other manly characteristics. *Real Men* . . . do what?

Paul tells the church in Corinth, "Be watchful, stand firm in the faith, *act like men*, be strong" (1 Corinthians 16:13, emphasis added). I love that verse. I hear it rev up the testosterone at men's rallies. But there's no footnote in my Bible explaining what activities define manliness. Does Paul mean we should know how to use a belt sander? take out the trash? drive a stick shift?

Ever get one of those forwarded e-mails, "A Man Should Be Able To . . ."? Here are a few examples of the seventy-five things we're supposed to be able to do, according to *Esquire* magazine (with my comments in parentheses):

→ Give advice that matters in one sentence. ("Don't count your chickens before they hatch" doesn't count; but try, "Everyone has the will to win, but few have the will to prepare to win." Classic, even if it is from Bobby Knight.)

→ Name a book that matters. (*Calvin and Hobbes* is not an option.)

→ Cook meat somewhere other than the grill. (Like the microwave?)

→ Throw a punch. (It's better to be a peacemaker, though.)

→ Calculate square footage. (Width x length, but don't ask for cubic length.)

→ Feign interest. (Most married guys already have this one down.)

→ Drive an eightpenny nail into a treated two-by-four without thinking about it. (Avoid your thumb, or it is all you will think about for the rest of the day.)

→ Speak a foreign language. (Your wife's dialect is a good place to start.)

→ Hit a jump shot in pool. (Or at least hit an occasional jump shot in basketball.)

→ Tell a joke. (Is it funny? Is it clean? If not, don't bother.)

→ Break another man's grip on [your] wrist. (Rotate your arm rapidly in the grip, toward the other guy's thumb, the author suggests. If that doesn't work, poke him in the eye with your free hand.)

→ Tell a woman's dress size. (Tread very carefully here!)

→ Sometimes, kick some _____. (I don't think he meant donkeys.)[1]

I wonder if that's what Paul had in mind when he said, "Act like men." What would you list? And could you live up to the expectations? I usually hate those lists because they typically talk a great deal about home repair. For some guys, handyman work involves circular saws and drywall mud. For me, it involves lightbulbs and air filters. I have a tool belt, but I only put it on when my father-in-law, who is a general contractor, comes to help me do all the things Jen thinks I should be able to do. Come to think of it, I'm pretty sure she's the one forwarding me those e-mails.

I've noticed, though, that none of those lists ever say things like this:

↝ Know a Bible verse other than John 3:16.

↝ Love Jesus more than your WaveRunner.

↝ Calculate your tithe before taxes.

↝ Once in a while, *you* arrange for the babysitter.

↝ Bring your wife flowers when it's not an anniversary or birthday.

↝ Pray for longer than ten seconds and about something other than safety for travel, healing for a relative, or "those people on the mission field."

↝ Sometimes, you gotta turn the other cheek.

After my voice finally stopped cracking and hair migrated to my armpits, no one gave me a manual on manhood. I once heard a good friend say, "In the absence of a definition, one will be given for you." It didn't take long for me to create my own definition of *manhood* with caricatures drawn from movies and television. Real men chiseled their bodies, rebuilt classic cars, and snagged beautiful women. In our culture, we've reduced manhood to strength, skills, and sex appeal.

I know I asked this earlier, but really, how would you define a real man? Write down your thoughts. Better yet, write down a name: Who do you know that embodies what it looks like to be a real man?[2]

Jesus far exceeds our culture's anemic and scattershot definition of manhood. He defines manhood more by a man's sacrifice than by his skills or strength or sex appeal. Jesus as a real man didn't snag beautiful women to make himself look good; he chose to love a bride into beauty and make her look good.

There's no doubt that Jesus fit many descriptions of the first list:

↝ Jesus gave advice that mattered in one sentence: "So whatever you wish that others would do to you, do also to them" (Matthew 7:12).

↝ He cooked meat over a campfire (John 21).

↝ He could name a book that mattered. (He quoted most often from Isaiah and Deuteronomy.)

→ As a carpenter, I bet he knew square footage and could drive an eightpenny nail without thinking about it.

→ He spoke a foreign language or two (Hebrew and Aramaic).

→ He didn't necessarily tell jokes, but he told some interesting parables with some pretty powerful punch lines.

→ When he confronted cheating money changers in the temple, he clearly kicked some . . . tables over.

In the apostle Paul's playbook for marriage, he calls out two fundamentals for how real men love their brides: "In the same way husbands should love their wives as their own bodies. He who loves his wife loves himself. For no one ever hated his own flesh, but *nourishes* and *cherishes* it, just as Christ does the church" (Ephesians 5:28–29, emphasis added). Just as star athletes never graduate from the fundamentals, husbands committed to beautifying their wives must practice the same drills over and over again. But notice what Paul says about these "drills": The key to loving our wives is to treat them with the same care that we treat ourselves—through *nourishing* and *cherishing*. Let's take a closer look at the first of these two words. We'll look at the second word in the next chapter.

Nourishing Love

The first fundamental guideline for husbands who want to love like Christ is to *provide nourishment*. I don't know about you, but I make it a policy not to miss a meal. I feed my body because it's *crucial to my survival*. I don't care if you can bench-press 400 pounds and make Tony Horton, the P90X guy, look flabby; your strength will fail without sustenance.

My provision of nourishment is also *consistent*. About every four hours—or less—I feed the beast. Unless I'm fasting for a short (very short!) period of time, there isn't a day that goes by when I don't enjoy some form of food—breakfast, lunch, *and* dinner.

Not only do I make sure to eat on a regular basis, but I also *cater to my tastes*. You're not going to catch me at the all-you-can-eat veggie and tofu bar. I prefer sizzling fajitas, deep-dish pizzas, burgers with toppings that drip down to my elbows, and a well-stocked Indian buffet. Unless I'm on the mission field, I eat what I love.

The same principles of nourishment apply to your marriage. I don't care if your relationship with your wife appears as solid as Tony Horton's six-pack abs, without *consistent* and *catered* sustenance for your bride, her strength will fail. Nourishment is *crucial* to the survival of your marriage.

Shortly after his resurrection, Jesus spoke at a men's breakfast. Actually, he showed up on the beach where some of his disciples were working and he built a fire, grilled some fish, baked some bread, and invited the disciples to join him. It was just after this meal that Jesus began to teach Peter what it means to love as Christ loved. After everyone had eaten their fill, Jesus looked at Peter and asked him the same question three times: "Simon, do you love me?"

Peter, who probably felt like the kid who is always at the principal's office, responded, "Yes, Lord, you know I love you." With each affirmation, Jesus issued an order: "Feed my lambs. . . . Tend my sheep. . . . Feed my sheep." (See John 21:15–19.)

With those three simple phrases, Jesus wrote Peter's job description for leading the church—and by implication, wrote the job description for every husband who says, "I do." In case Peter ever wondered what it looked like to love Christ's bride— the church—he could look up on any hillside in Palestine and see a shepherd leading a flock. The shepherd nourished the sheep *consistently*. He *catered* the food to their bodies' needs. And this provision was *crucial* to their survival.

Many women feel malnourished by their husbands. Their closets may be stuffed with clothes and their pantries stocked with food, but their souls are famished for consistent nourishment, without which their strength for the marriage will fail.

Nourishment Is Crucial

If you get a chance, pick up two short, but abundantly insightful, books, *For Men Only* and *For Women Only* by Shaunti and Jeff Feldhahn. Reading these books is like sneaking a peek at the opposing team's playbook before a game. Each volume breaks down the strengths, weaknesses, patterns, and plays that we run as husbands and wives. The Feldhahns do a brilliant job of understanding how men and women think, and why we act the way we act. In short, every man wants to be *praised*, and every woman wants to be *pursued*.

Virtually every husband has a latent insecurity. He continually asks himself, in some form or fashion, "Am I strong enough? Am I capable?" By the same token, virtually every wife has her own latent insecurity. She continually asks herself, "Am I still loved? Am I worth pursuing?"

During the courtship period, you don't have to tell a guy to pursue a girl. That's as natural as eating. But after he says, "I do," his thinking changes. Whether consciously or not, his attitude is one of "mission accomplished." In his mind, he closed the deal, bagged the kill, or broke the tape, and he's ready for the next challenge. But a wife isn't a closed deal, a trophy on the wall, or a finish line.

Jeff Feldhahn asks, "Have you ever wondered why your wife asks 'Do you love me?' even though you've done nothing to indicate you've changed your mind about loving her? (In fact, you just told her you loved her this morning on the way out the door!)" Or why she "takes your need for space or 'cave' time as an indication you're upset with and trying to get away from her?" Or why she "wants to talk, talk, talk about your relationship, . . . [or] seems to turn critical or pushy for no reason you can figure?" Buried in these perplexing behaviors are the questions every wife is asking: "Do you still love me? Are we still okay?"[3]

According to the Feldhahns, seven out of ten women said that how their husbands felt about them was on their minds "occasionally" to "nearly always." Our wives want to know: Am I still an open deal? a trophy to be sought? a race yet to run?

When Paul says, "Husbands, love your wives" (Ephesians 5:25), he's speaking in the present active indicative tense. That simply means it's an *ongoing* action. Never ending. Constant pursuit. Continual care. No finish line. Just as we cannot imagine an infant surviving without continual nourishment from its mother, Paul cannot imagine a wife surviving without continual emotional nourishment from her husband.

When Jen breast-fed our three kids, I don't ever remember a conversation like this . . .

"Honey, when was the last time you fed the kids?"

"Oh, I don't know, maybe a couple of days ago."

No, she made sure their needs were met. Throughout the day, she set aside her own agenda to satisfy their appetites. At night, she interrupted her sleep for their sustenance. I remember seeing her stumble out of bed and thinking, *Man, I'm glad God didn't issue that equipment to me.* If I asked you the question, When was the last time you nourished your wife's heart by interrupting your agenda to win her affections? would you respond by saying, "Oh, I don't know, maybe a couple weeks ago?" A husband's love and affection is every bit as crucial to his wife's survival as a mother's milk is to a baby's. It's just a natural part of the way things work.

It's easy for me to hit the snooze button on feeding Jen's heart, especially if I'm feeling like I'm on her bad side. I might feel as if she is being overly critical, difficult, or pushing me away. Jeff Feldhahn admits what I've often experienced: "I can't tell you how many times when facing resistance I've thought, *Fine, suit yourself. I've got to go cut the lawn anyway.* And then I pretty much put the incident out of my mind. Unfortunately, she can't. She's still seeking the answer to the original question: 'Do you still love me?'"[4]

It's also easy to hit the snooze button when things seem to be going smoothly. I imagine that because I provide for her basic physical needs—food, clothing, and shelter—I'm meeting her needs. But that's not the same thing as providing for her emotional and relational nourishment. As Shaunti Feldhahn points out, "It's irrelevant whether she should 'know logically' that she's loved. If she doesn't *feel* loved, it's the same for her as if she *isn't* loved."[5]

If I start believing that my love is as crucial to my wife as mother's milk is to a baby, I'll interrupt my agenda to satisfy her appetite. I'll sacrifice my comfort for her care. And I'll do whatever it takes to identify the specific nourishment she needs.

Nourishment Is Catered

A nursing baby has a limited menu: mother's milk. But as the baby continues to grow, its palate expands as well. Applied to marriage, this means that what satisfies your wife's need for love and affection won't always be the same. As your relationship grows and matures, her needs will change as well. You can't just rest on your laurels; it's a continual and progressive pursuit. That said, how do we know if our wives feel pursued and loved by us? Your guess is as good as mine. I think that's why Peter says, "Husbands, live with your wives *in an understanding way*" (1 Peter 3:7, emphasis added). He knows we may never understand, but God holds us accountable to try.

Gary Chapman, author of the classic relationship book *The Five Love Languages*, is one of the best marriage coaches out there. He says if you want to discover what nourishes your wife's heart, listen to her irritations: "My spouse's criticisms about my behavior provide me with the clearest clue to her primary love language. People tend to criticize their spouse most loudly in the area where they themselves have the deepest emotional need." In other words, turn criticisms into clues. Chapman adds that "criticism often needs clarification." After a tirade you might want to ask her, "It sounds like that is extremely important to you. Could you explain why it is so crucial?"[6] Next time you notice your wife's evil eyes, start taking notes. After you get over your hurt feelings, you'll see a grocery list of nourishing things you can do and say to feed your wife's heart. Man, I wish someone would have dropped me this clue on my wedding day!

When I came home late again and Jen threw the flowers on the kitchen table and said, "You just don't get it, do you?" she volunteered the answer to the question I didn't know enough to ask. (But, guys, it rarely works that way.) She said, "Instead of buying me flowers that will die in a few days, why not just use that time to get home earlier?" She was giving me a big, fat clue that her primary love language was *quality time*, to put it in Gary Chapman's terms. Don't get me wrong; she appreciates flowers and gifts, but she feels most loved when I set aside my own agenda to spend time with her.

When Jen was growing up, her dad came home every night at 5:30 and spent the rest of the evening with his family. My dad came home between 6:00 and 6:30, and then would often go out for an evening meeting. So when I told Jen I'd be home around six, in my mind I had a thirty-minute window. In Jen's mind, it was more like thirty seconds. I've learned that the earlier I can let her know when I'm going to be late, the easier it is for her to adapt. Knowing her primary love language saves me a world of grief. It also gives me a book of plays to run. Jen feels pursued when I spend time with her; when I schedule a lunch with her; when I eat dinner with her without looking at texts or e-mails; and when I turn off my phone on my day off. For Jen, quality time means focused, quantity time.

Not long ago, I asked some friends' wives when they felt most loved by their husbands. Here are some of their responses:

→ When he takes me to Starbucks, and then we drive out of the city, maybe just to a small neighboring community, for a quiet lunch. By doing this, he gives me his undivided attention. We truly talk about things. He'll engage me with questions, such as, "What's going on in our lives? How can we better handle situations? What are we doing right? Wrong? Where do we go from here? What are you feeling? What can I help you with?"

→ When he occasionally meets me for lunch and does a pretty good job of not looking at his BlackBerry. It makes me feel valued, because he's taking time out of his busy day to just sit and listen or help me "fix" an issue.

→ He puts me first, many times, even down to who gets the last piece of pizza or dessert!

→ I feel special when he watches the kids when they wake up at five or six, so I can sleep a little bit longer. Also, I feel special when he plans something for us to do together.

→ Another treasure is a cup of tea on weekend mornings—whether it be a home chore day or a running-around Saturday or Sunday, I come to the kitchen and often find a steamy mug of tea with honey, without having asked for it. Sometimes some cinnamon toast, too. . . . I must confess I have seen this before—for as long as I can remember, my husband has always treated his mother to the same extras when we visit her. Thankfully, in my home it's true what they say about watching how a man treats his mother, because it shows how he will value his wife.

→ Going to my mother's house, because he does not consider that a vacation.

→ Doing simple chores without being asked.

→ He plans dates for us and even lines up the sitter.

→ He calls me his "bride" and always compliments my appearance, even if I look like warmed-over death.

→ After fourteen years of marriage and two kids, he makes me feel like a newlywed when he pulls me close, looks into my eyes and says, "I love you so much," and leads me into a slow dance across the kitchen floor.

→ If he leaves the house at an unreasonable hour in the morning, he calls me later from work every day just to say, "I love you."

→ He may not want me to say this, but . . . he cleans the bathrooms. I can't believe that God let me find a man who would do this. I utterly despise this task—and my college roommates have plenty of stories they could tell!

→ He tells me he loves me daily.

→ My hubby brings me coffee in bed almost every morning. It's a very simple gesture, but there is nothing like knowing he thinks to do that for me every morning.

→ Even though I don't believe it, he thinks I'm pretty.

→ He buys me pots and pans for Christmas—not just any pots and pans, but the All-Clad Master Chef Series 2.

Did you notice how different the answers are? (That last one is from Jen. I'm betting if you bought your wife a pot for Christmas, she'd use it as a weapon. But Jen's passion is cooking. She felt loved because I fueled that passion.) Guys, the playbook is not hard to find on this one. You can either take notes from your wife's rants, or you can just ask her what she likes. You will get the results either way, but one way is far less painful. If you have the guts, you can simply ask her a very risky question: "Honey, do you feel the depth of my love?" (Not, "Do you know I love you?" but, "Do you *feel* it?") If she says no, ask her, "How can I help you *feel* my love for you?" Then be ready to take some notes!

Nourishment Is Consistent

One of the great ironies in my life is that I can't remember Scripture but I can remember the chorus to "Achy Breaky Heart." Plain and simple, we remember what's repeated. For example, let's see if you can finish the following sentences, which you no doubt heard countless times while growing up:

If you don't stop crying, _____.
A little soap and water _____.
Always wear clean underwear, _____.

If you answered, ". . . I'll give you something to cry about," ". . . never hurt anyone," and ". . . in case you get in an accident," then you grew up in a household similar to mine. I have to admit, though, that last one baffles me. I've never heard a traffic reporter, flying over an accident scene, say, "We're at the scene of a thirty-car pileup on I-85. Traffic is backed up for miles, but we just received confirmation that everyone involved was wearing clean underwear."

We remember hit songs and sitcom dialogue from our childhoods. Some—like the chorus to "Achy Breaky Heart"—we wish we could purge from our memory banks.

Memorizing Scripture is valuable because it embeds in our minds the songs that God the Father sings to his children as a reminder of his presence. The prophet Zephaniah says, "Your God is present among you, a strong Warrior there to save you.

Happy to have you back, he'll calm you with his love and delight you with his songs" (Zephaniah 3:17 MSG).

You may not remember all the lyrics of the Bible, but you don't have to read long to hear the choruses God sings again and again to his kids:

→ Be strong and courageous
→ Fear not
→ I have loved you with an everlasting love

I find two constant insecurities in my life: feeling unaffirmed and fearing the unknown. Yet the Lord affirms over and over again that I am loved. He repeatedly reminds me to be strong and courageous. Even though I know these things are true, I need to hear them over and over again so I won't forget. God sings these repeated choruses to nourish the deepest needs of our hearts.

The chorus a woman sings to herself every day goes something like this: "Mirror, mirror on the wall, am I fairer to him after all?" One of a woman's deepest needs is to know that her husband finds her beautiful. The Feldhahns found that more than three out of four women under the age of forty-five felt this need. Among women thirty-five and younger, the percentage rose to 84 percent. No matter how successful, self-assured, or stylish a woman is; no matter how long she's been married; no matter how many times she's heard from others, "You are gorgeous!"; no matter how young or old she is; every wife needs to hear one chorus from her husband on a consistent basis: "You are beautiful."[7]

Every day, I sing a chorus to my ten-year-old daughter. As often as I can, I say, "Don't forget. You're beautiful." Sometimes I just shorten it to "Don't forget." She smiles—or now that she's in double digits, she just sighs. Sometimes before a business trip, I'll write her a card and find a way to slip in the chorus. I'll drop a note in her lunch box. I reflect her beauty because I know a day is coming when she will start measuring herself against different mirrors. She'll see beauty reflected back to her in the media and on the cover of magazines. She'll see her boyfriend dart his eyes when a scantily clad girl walks by. She'll notice pimples on her face looking like a constellation. Everywhere in our image-obsessed culture, she will face countless comparisons. I want her to remember that her dad reflects the one mirror that matters: "As a child of God, I am beautiful."

When you got married, one of God's precious daughters came to live with you. Not only that, but God placed you in a position of representing his love for her through you. That's why husbands are told to love as Christ loved. You have the power to either reflect your wife's beauty back to her, or cloud the mirror. Jeff Feldhahn mentions a few fundamental facts:

→ In our marriage, whether I find her beautiful may or may not be foremost in my mind, but it is an everyday (even if subconscious) issue for her.
→ In our house, there's really only one mirror. And that mirror is me.
→ Every day, I can reflect back to her the words she so needs to hear. But if I don't, I leave her vulnerable to both her inner questions and external pressure from an intimidating world.[8]

I've heard that men look at a mirror and see themselves twenty pounds lighter than they really are. Women look at a mirror and see themselves twenty pounds heavier. They need a new mirror. The reason I can't get "Don't break my heart, my achy, breaky heart" out of my mind is because it played on the radio countless times each day. Choruses are remembered because they are repeated, whether you want to hear them or not. For a man to reflect his wife's beauty, he must commit to singing choruses, whether he wants to or not. Every man composes choruses daily, with or without words. Your verbal praise reinforces your wife's beauty, and your silence makes her question her beauty. Remember Don and Sally from chapter 3? After more than three decades of marriage and four kids, Sally said, "Don still thinks I'm beautiful, even though I know what I look like in the mirror." In other words, day in and day out, during weight gain and weight loss, pregnancies and empty nest, evenings in cocktail dresses and mornings in gray sweats, new hairstyles and bed-head, Don reflected Sally's beauty so clearly that it altered whatever picture she saw in the mirror. Solomon said, "Death and life are in the power of the tongue" (Proverbs 18:21). You can nourish your wife with your words or bring death by your silence. In another book, Solomon dispels any insecurities his wife may have had about her body: "You are altogether beautiful, my love; *there is no flaw in you*" (Song of Solomon 4:7, emphasis added).

When I was in high school, Jim, my youth pastor, introduced his fiancée, Leslie, as "the most beautiful woman in the history of mankind." We rolled our eyes and I thought, *That line will last until he ties the knot.* A few years after Jim was married, he and I went out to a mall together. In the course of our shopping, he spoke to a sales clerk who obviously thought he was on the market. After she had sent a few subtle flirts his way, Jim whipped out his organizer, in which he carried a picture of Leslie, and said, "Can I introduce you to the most beautiful woman in the history of mankind?" Leslie is now in her forties and they have four kids, but Jim's story hasn't changed one iota. In fact, my dad still lives near Jim and Leslie, and he told me recently that he heard Jim's teenage sons introduce their mom as "the most beautiful woman in the history of mankind."

Jim trained himself to sing a chorus to his wife when she walked out in stilettos and a silky black dress and when she shuffled out in slippers and a maternity shirt. Regardless of the images flashed across the television set, or shouted from magazine covers, or how Leslie looked in the mirror, Jim nourished his wife's self-worth by repeating one simple phrase. We may forget the rest of the lyrics, but we don't forget the chorus.

Your wife may not want to hear one phrase repeated over decades, but she needs to hear some choruses about her beauty. For things to be remembered, they must be spoken. They must be specific. And they must be repeated. Come up with a few phrases and start working them into your daily routine.

→ In the middle of your workday, text one to your wife.

→ On a day that's not an anniversary, write one on a note and leave it where she'll be sure to find it.

→ In the middle of an argument, remind her that even though she irritates you, she still radiates beauty.

→ Calendar a compliment. When you plan out your week, write in "2 pm. Wed. Sing Chorus to my wife." She'll think you spontaneously thought of her. Don't give away your trade secrets.

→ Before you make love, describe to your wife in detail why you find her beautiful. If you need help, spend some time in Song of Solomon 4:1–16 and 7:1–9. Solomon compliments every part of his wife's body, from head to toe. Just remember that some of the phrases don't translate well from ancient Hebrew culture to our own. I wouldn't recommend using "your belly is a heap of wheat" or "your nose is like a tower of Lebanon."

Here's another risky question. Ask your bride, "Do you feel beautiful in my eyes? If not, how can I communicate better how lovely you are?" Unfortunately, many men—either by their silence, or by gawking at other women or peering at pornography—shatter the mirror without saying anything bad about their wives. We can't avoid the images that bombard us daily in the media, but we *can* decide what we look at, and we *can* choose to reflect our wives' beauty and to battle for purity in our minds. We'll come back to this topic in the next chapter.

Paul got it right with a simple chorus: *Care for your wife the same way you care for yourself.* Men nourish their own bodies instinctively. No one has to convince us to eat. I'm about to grab something in a few minutes. Great athletes understand the power of proper nourishment. I know countless guys who love to compete in triathlons, pound the weights, shoot hoops, and play sports. They instinctively know that without the right fuel, they bonk. Simply apply the same principle to your wife's emotional nourishment and you'll build her up and strengthen your marriage at the same time.

Here's a good line for our "Real Men" list: A real husband who loves like Jesus doesn't let his marriage bonk. He realizes that his bride's nourishment must be consistent and catered to her needs, because it's crucial to her survival (and to the survival and strength of the marriage).

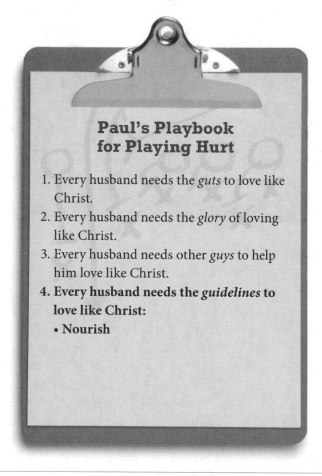

Paul's Playbook for Playing Hurt

1. Every husband needs the *guts* to love like Christ.
2. Every husband needs the *glory* of loving like Christ.
3. Every husband needs other *guys* to help him love like Christ.
4. **Every husband needs the *guidelines* to love like Christ:**
   • **Nourish**

THE HOT SEAT

1. What's your wife's passion? How do you find ways for her to explore and enjoy that passion? How can you interrupt your agenda to help her express herself and enjoy the gifts God has given her?

2. How did your wife respond to those two risky questions? If you haven't asked her yet, ask her now.

   a. Do you feel the depth of my love? If not, how can I help you feel it?

   b. Do you feel beautiful in my eyes? If not, how can I communicate that better?

3. What's one way of nourishing your wife that you will implement this week?

4. Write down a few "choruses" you can sing to your wife. Start singing, man!

Chapter 7

Become a Thermostat, Not a Thermometer

IF YOU'RE LIKE ME (and like most husbands), you can take your wife's emotional temperature from about twenty feet away. When Jen is hot (I don't mean ready to slip between the sheets with me), I know to seek out a cooler climate, perhaps out on the back deck with an iced tea. When she's cold, I look for a warmer personality—like the TV—to keep me company. I'm not saying these responses are right. I'm just saying that's what I tend to do. But Paul, in his playbook for marriage, calls us to *set* the emotional climate in our homes, not just measure it.

After providing constant and catered nourishment that is crucial for our brides, the second fundamental for a winning marriage is to *cherish* our wives. It's a word that can mean "bring warmth to," and from which we derive our words *thermal* and *thermostat*. Paul says we instinctively cherish our own bodies (Ephesians 5:29). If it's hot, we put on our sandals and crank up the AC. If it's cold, we look for our fuzzy socks and build a fire. When Paul tells us to love our wives as we love our own bodies

(Ephesians 5:28), he's encouraging us to *cherish* their emotional needs in the same way we cherish our own physical needs. If she's chilly, it's our job to warm her up. If she's steaming, then we need to help her lower the mercury. In other words, the call to *cherish* means we have to engage when we'd rather shrink back.

Whenever I'm irritated with someone, my natural inclination is to pull away. It happens with my bride, and, incidentally, it happened with Jesus' bride. The whole book of Ephesians was written because two groups of people retreated from each other (Ephesians 2:14–22). Sitting in the pews of Ephesus were Gentiles and Jews. That may mean little to a twenty-first century mindset, but imagine segregationist whites in the 1950s sitting next to African Americans. Segregationists tolerated other races just as long as they stayed in their separate world. Back in Ephesus, the Gentiles and Jews found themselves on the same team wearing the same uniform. Because of Jesus, two starkly different people became one. Soon after the church was founded, a theological argument threatened their oneness. Mistrust and irritation crept in. Rather than pursue reconciliation, they retreated toward isolation. Paul reminded them, "I . . . urge you to walk in a manner worthy of the calling to which you have been called, with all humility and gentleness, with patience, bearing with one another in love, eager to maintain the unity of the Spirit in the bond of peace. There is one body and one Spirit—just as you were called to the one hope that belongs to your call" (4:1–4). "I urge you" has the force of "I'm pleading with you!" In other words, Paul said, "You two were made into one—so live like it!"

When you said, "I do," two starkly different people became one. Oneness doesn't mean sameness. The Gentiles loved bacon-wrapped shellfish and the Jews ate whitefish; the Gentiles worked seven days on, no days off; the Jews kicked up their heels on Saturdays. Jews and Gentiles ate different, looked different, acted different, and probably cheered for different teams. Yet Jesus made them one in spirit and body.

It's amazing how quickly your whole body responds when you get a sliver in your finger. Your nerves shoot pain warnings to your brain. Like missile lock, your eyes fix on the problem. Your legs halt any movement. Your other digits start trying to dig out the intruder. Proportionately the sliver affects a small surface area, but your whole body springs into action. I wish that was true in marriage. When a sliver of bitterness or frustration enters my marriage, the whole body should work to get it out. But all too often, I let it fester.

In our playbook Paul wrote, "In the same way husbands should love their wives as their own bodies. He who loves his wife loves himself. For no one ever hated his own flesh, but nourishes and cherishes it, just as Christ does the church, because we are *members of his body*" (Ephesians 5:28–30, emphasis added). Translation: When I nourish Jen, I nourish myself because our relationship flourishes. When I cherish Jen, I cherish myself. When I hurt Jen or allow pain to fester, I shoot myself in the foot.

That's the frustrating part of oneness; when I punish Jen with the silent treatment, I jack up my blood pressure. If I pout to win her pity, I just look like a third grader. If I yell at her, I hurt my heart. If I ignore her irritation, it irritates me more. Even if I try, I can't tear apart what God has joined (Matthew 19:6). That's why Paul continued his playbook by quoting Genesis 2:24: "Therefore a man shall leave his father and his mother and hold fast to his wife, and they shall become one flesh."

God's original intent for marriage: "Oneness." Two becoming one. If it doesn't mean "sameness," what does it mean? God illustrates oneness with the first couple in the garden of Eden, "And the man and his wife were both naked and were not ashamed" (Genesis 2:25). Though many definitions abound for oneness, I think a simple way to describe it is *living with each other without hiding from each other*. Not only did Adam and Eve bare everything physically to one another, they were unashamed of their thoughts, actions, and desires. They had nothing to hide.

It doesn't take long for something to threaten our oneness. A husband comes home late again and asks his wife, "What's wrong?" She hides her true emotions by saying, "Nothing, *I'm fine*." He knows she's not, but it's just not worth the hassle. A wife notices another sideways glance at a short skirt in the mall,

"Hey, what were you looking at?" He hides his shame by saying, "Nothing, just window shopping." She knows he's lying, but neither want to address the topic. When do you grab fig leaves and hide your real thoughts, actions, and desires? For me, it's easy to hide in three areas: When it comes to conflict resolution, I hide behind my *irritation*. When it comes to spiritual leadership, I hide behind my *intimidation*. When it comes to sexual intimacy, I hide behind my *illicit desires*. In those moments, even if I'm physically present, I'm hiding from Jen rather than living with Jen. Rather than walk toward our "calling" to be one, I shrink back. And I hear God in the back of my mind, "I made you two into one—so live like it!"

Cherish Her by Resolving Conflict

As men, we're prone to short-circuit intimacy with our wives by settling for harmony—or a reasonable facsimile thereof. The problem is that what passes for harmony is often glossed-over unresolved conflict. We would rather hide behind our irritation than press for resolution. When our tendency is to pull back instead of engage, we leave our wives feeling uncherished, unnourished, and unloved.

Several years ago, at a time when we were in transition (translation, I had lost my job), a job opened up in Atlanta. Jen and I took a long weekend and drove down from Charlotte to check things out. After talking to the company and looking around the area, I felt strongly about moving forward. Better income. Bigger influence. Brighter future. And I needed a job. Jen felt just as strongly that it wasn't the right decision. From her perspective, we could uproot our kids for the third time in five years, or I could just tear out her heart without anesthesia. I didn't know what to say to that kind of response, so I didn't say anything. During the entire three-hour drive back to North Carolina, I might have uttered a single sentence: "What do you want your kids to eat for dinner?"

All the way home, I abdicated my responsibility to engage my wife, and I abused her with my silence. I heard my heavenly Coach call me out multiple times:

"Goins, that's my daughter over there you're treating like a leper."

"You may be right, but you're treating her wrong."

"You see her wilting. It's time to get off the bench and back in the game."

Instead of playing hurt, I fell back on my usual strategies. I mentally drew up depositions to *persuade* her to my perspective, while I used my silence to *punish* her to perfection. When we went to bed that night, I tried in vain to purge the chorus that Paul was singing in my ear: "Don't let the sun go down on your anger." For us, the sun had already set. Barely six inches apart, we slept in different galaxies.

In those moments when I'm irritated by something Jen has said or done, or we're at loggerheads with each other over a decision, I care very little about victory in my marriage; I just want justice for my injuries. When my expectations have been blown, my rights have been trampled, or my emotions have been hurt, conflict usually causes one of two reactions: either I abdicate my responsibility to repair the breach, or I find a way to punish Jen for the conflict.

I've always been a stuffer. I bury my real emotions somewhere back in the sock drawer of my heart. I'd rather have a semblance of harmony than dig deep and truly resolve our disagreements. Jen and I happen to be good enough friends that it's easy to let contentious discussions fade away in favor of "keeping the peace." If you ignore something long enough, eventually the negative feelings pass. And when you have kids, new distractions quickly push unresolved issues to the sidelines. Having children is great way to get your mind off your marriage. But those unresolved conflicts have a way of bubbling back to the surface—usually at the worst possible moment.

Winning marriages are ones where the couple has learned how to resolve conflict rather than constantly sweeping it under the rug. The essence of playing hurt is being willing to get off the bench when we'd rather sit and nurse our injuries. To engage when we'd rather retreat. To pursue when we'd rather pout.

I avoid conflict because I'm afraid to express my true feelings and risk a response that I can't handle. And I've learned over the years that, given enough time, our relationship will cool back to normal. We get lulled into thinking the area's been cleared—and then we step on another land mine and we're right back in the middle of the war zone. Left to fester, those unresolved conflicts will eventually erupt like a shaken can of soda.

When we got married, God called us to reflect his love to our spouse—to love an imperfect person unconditionally for a lifetime. Godly love requires us to move forward when we'd prefer to run away. A note in *The Nelson Study Bible* captures the essence of godly, unconditional love:

> This word, *agape*, describes a love that is based on the deliberate choice of the one who loves rather than the worthiness of the one who is loved. This kind of love goes against natural human inclination. It is a giving, selfless, expect-nothing-in-return kind of love. . . .
>
> Our modern, "throw-away" society encourages us to get rid of people in our lives who are difficult to get along with, whether they are friends, family, or acquaintances. Yet this attitude runs in complete contrast to the love described by Paul. True love puts up with people who would be easier to give up on.[1]

Agape love is impossible unless we've been hurt. Lucky for us, marriage provides many wonderful opportunities to get hurt. On top of that, our enemy—our real enemy, the devil—prowls around looking for opportunities to devour us. He tries to stir up fear and discord to keep us from moving forward and resolving our conflicts.

When we're hiding behind fear and pain, we need some strategies to get us off the bench and back in the game. I've discovered a simple, three-step process that gets me moving forward when my natural inclination is to run away. Let's call it the ABC play: *Ask, Blink, Commit.*

Ask

Ask God to search your heart and unmask your issues (Psalm 139:23–24). The last thing we're inclined to do in the middle of a conflict is turn the magnifying glass back on ourselves. But marriages that have a high success rate are ones in which the spouses are far more aware of the damage done to the other person than the damage the other person has done to them. Even if you think the problem is 99 percent your wife's fault, you can still own up to your 1 percent (which is probably a lot bigger than 1 percent—trust me). Remember, injuries in marriage affect our eyesight. We get focused on the wrong things and the real enemy gets blurred. Though Jen could have done a far better job of recognizing my desire to provide for our family, I let her obvious irritation over moving dictate my feelings toward her. I started seeking retribution over reconciliation.

Blink

Be willing to blink first. Whether your conflicts are characterized by silence or shouting, someone has to break the impasse.

Staring contests are cute when you're a kid. As a strategy for resolving conflict with a spouse, they're only cruel. After that eternal van ride from Atlanta to Charlotte, I wish I could say I blinked first. But the next morning, after the kids went to school, Jen disarmed me with a simple apology: "Brian, I'm sorry for how I treated you yesterday. I'm confident you'll listen to God on this decision and I'm willing to follow you." Boy, did that catch me off guard.

What? I thought. *No, I'm prepped! I have my depositions rehearsed! I'm ready to start my opening argument!*

Jen owned up to her 1 percent, leaving me to deal with my 99 percent. Though her desires hadn't changed, her attitude toward me had done a 180. She opened the door to oneness by letting the gloves drop.

We ended up not moving, but not because Jen persuaded me through pouting. When I woke up the next morning, with the unresolved conflict still churning in my gut, I was ready to move just to spite her! (How's that for a mature attitude and unconditional love?) But because she cared more about victory for our marriage than vindication for herself, she opened the door to an honest dialogue that helped us untangle the issue from our emotions.

The hardest thing about blinking first is that the time to do it is right in the middle of the conflict. For men in particular, not backing down is a point of pride. But when we bow up, we're just hiding behind our fear and anger. God calls us to a different standard. He calls us to love our wives as Christ loved the church—that is, to give ourselves up for her. Here are some ways I've learned to blink in the middle of an argument:

1. *Blink with a Reality Check.* Try to untangle your emotions from the issue with clarifying statements: "We're obviously irritated with each other. But it's not helping us, our kids, or the problem for us to stay mad. What is it we're fighting about again?"

2. *Blink with Reinforcement.* Reinforce the relationship with reminders of your lasting commitment despite the current conflict: "I just want you to know that even though we're both irritated, I want to get back to intimacy. I love you. And more than anything, I want victory over this problem."

3. *Blink with Prayer.* I know it sounds pious, but remember: your battle is not against flesh and blood. The enemy is working overtime to exploit the wedge in your marriage. The Bible says, "Capture every thought . . ." Ask the Spirit of God to temper your tongues and direct your thoughts.

4. *Blink with an Apology.* Refuse to engage in a battle of returning insult for insult (following Christ's example, see 1 Peter 2:21–24). Instead, examine and own up to your part in the conflict. Trust God to change a heart. Nothing disarms like owning your part of the argument. God can use an apology to calm stormy currents.

Commit

Finally, commit to finding best practices for dealing with conflict. Pick up some books at the bookstore or check them out at the library. Download one on your Kindle.[2] Take a marriage coach or a "cairn" husband out to lunch—someone who can help you discover what works. Chances are you learned how couples fight by watching your parents. If they fought fair and successfully resolved their conflicts, you have a good role model to follow. If not—if you grew up watching your mom and dad shouting or sulking—you'll have to look elsewhere.

Don't be afraid to expand your search beyond the borders of marriage and family relationships. Whether you realize it or not, you're probably already an expert at resolving conflict. Men successfully fight every day without damaging relationships. They fight with racquets. They contest each other on the basketball court. They spar in boxing rings. They race in triathlons. They may not always win, but they still walk away from the battle as friends because they agree on the rules before the contest. That's one reason I love the book *Fight Fair* by Tim and Joy Downs. It's a great, quick read about how to set up ground rules before the altercation begins.

Imagine if you and your wife brought a bunch of yellow flags into your next verbal tussle. You throw a flag when she starts going down her laundry list of complaints: "False start. Only one issue can move at a time!" She throws a flag when you bring up something that happened a year ago: "Delay of game. Time ran out on that topic 360 days ago!" You wave your hands to stop the action: "Too many men on the field. No references to in-laws allowed in this conversation!"

Establishing rules helps you and your wife untangle emotions from issues and work toward a mutually satisfying solution. A smart man doesn't wait for the rain to come before he fixes a broken roof. He repairs it when the sun is shining. If your conflict resolution is broken, repair the breaches before the rain starts. Set up the ground rules. When the mercury starts to rise again in your relationship, you will have far more confidence to adjust the thermostat rather than slip away to your man cave while your wife cools down on her own.

Cherish Her by Leading Spiritually

What do you think of when you hear the term, "spiritual leadership"? Might as well try to define a political independent. When I look at the highlights from Jesus' life, I see a spiritual leader who consistently initiated spiritual conversations about God and with God (prayer). For many of us, I think it's far easier to talk about everything else except God: the job, the kids, the house, the Tar Heels, the television. For many husbands, leading spiritually looks like starting the ignition and driving everyone to church. As a pastor, I'm for church attendance but not for outsourcing our role as spiritual leader in the home. Rather than engaging our wives spiritually we hide behind our *intimidation.*

I remember the first time I went out for football. As you know from my stories about crew, no one mistook me for a lineman. The coach put me at outside linebacker. On a running play, my job was to contain the left side of the field and pursue on plays to the right. On the first snap at practice, everything happened so fast. Before I could read the play, the quarterback had already given up the ball and the running back was five yards downfield. I did my best statue impression until the quarterback, a Pop Warner vet, saw me and decided to teach me a lesson about giving up on a play before the whistle blows. Next thing I knew, I was flat on the ground looking up at my laughing teammate. I had two thoughts at that moment: *I have no idea what I'm doing*, and *I don't think I'm cut out for this sport.*

I think many men want to lead spiritually in their homes, but they get out on the field and are not quite sure how the play is supposed to work, or they get knocked down by guilt and think: *I have no idea what I'm doing. I'm probably not cut out for this sport.* Rather than fight through the intimidation, many husbands shrink back. Frankly, it's easier to be the taxi driver to church than to be the spiritual driver in the home.

In Paul's playbook for marriage, he imagines Jesus leading his bride through the ceremonial bath before their wedding, "that he might sanctify her, having cleansed her by the washing of water with the word" (Ephesians 5:26). Weird phrase, but it's important that we understand this word picture, because Paul says, "In the same way husbands should love their wives" (Ephesians 5:28).

When Jesus spoke to his disciples on the night before his death, he told them, "Already you are clean because of the word that I have spoken to you" (John 15:3). That same night he prayed for his disciples, "Sanctify them in the truth; your word is truth" (John 17:17). The *word* of God cleanses. As Jesus taught and led his disciples in the way of truth, he "cleansed" them, set them apart, and prepared them to become his bride—the church. In the same way, a husband is called to lead his wife with the Word of God. As he does so, he "cleanses" her and sets her apart and prepares to present her back to God for his service.

I don't remember my dad ever sitting our family down for devotions. We prayed together, but usually right before we passed the potatoes. And I don't say that to blame my dad. About the only thing his dad had modeled for him was how to make moonshine and yell at his mom. My dad reversed the curse of abuse and alcoholism in his home. He advanced the ball downfield the best way he knew how.

My parents started taking us kids to church when I was eight. I know my dad heard, "You're the spiritual leader in the home. You need to lead." I know he got the call from the Coach, "Hey, get in the game." But I think he probably felt much like I did after getting knocked on my keister at football practice: I have no idea what I'm doing and I don't think I'm cut out for this sport.

That pattern continued with me. I remember when Jen said, "Why is it you pray with other guys, but not with me?" I've been to Promise Keepers, read *Wild at Heart*, studied and even taught Men's Fraternity; but regardless of what I know is right, I still trip over the same hurdle: my own fears.

Watching old westerns, I never heard John Wayne say, "All right, little lady, we better ask God to protect us before those cowpokes come and attack the farm." In *Braveheart*, when William Wallace yells to his outmatched countrymen, "They may take our lives, but they'll never take OUR FREEDOM!" he doesn't add, "Now, let's bow in prayer before we slaughter the English." Despite the bumper stickers, the real men we idolize don't pray. They don't love Jesus. They barely give him a second thought.

Spiritual leadership might be one of the most intimidating things about being a husband. Though there are countless books, daily devotionals, and podcasts on the subject, resources alone won't help us get over our insecurities. Once again, this is where a good coach and teammates come into play. Rather than retreating to the bench, figure out how to overcome the obstacles and stay in the game. Learn from guys who are leading their families well. Get together with other men and share your scars in this area. Battle together. You'll be surprised at how many guys have felt at one time or another that they weren't cut out for this sport! Few men I know started their marriage knowing how to lead spiritually. But they found the right "and" guys, stepped out in faith, and watched God honor their effort.

Even as a pastor, it's easier to stand up and preach a sermon, and assume that fulfills my responsibility to provide spiritual leadership, than to lead Jen and my kids actively at home. One thing that helped me start praying with Jen was realizing that I don't have to *perform* for her. It's not the length of the prayer or the eloquence of the words that counts; it's simply talking together with our heavenly Father. Jen does not expect me to give her a theological lecture about Scripture. She just wants me to let her in on the conversations I'm having with God. When chaos hits our home because of a lost job, struggles with the kids, or unexpected bills, she'd much rather have me pull over and ask God for directions (sound familiar?) than drive endlessly around the block trying to solve the problem on my own. A quick two- or three-minute prayer about our need for God's wisdom sets her mind more at ease than two or three hours of stress and planning.

Cherish Your Bride More Than You Chase Bubbles

Let's talk about sex. Specifically, let's talk about the 12-minute gap. Why in the world would God design men to reach orgasm in about 2.8 minutes and women in about 14 minutes?[3] As we said earlier, oneness does not mean sameness. Nowhere is this more visible than when a husband and wife are naked. Not only do we look physically different but we experience sexual pleasure in different ways, and, according to the gap, at different speeds. Let me state the obvious: every man enjoys orgasm, but that's not the height of his sexual pleasure. As a mentor told me once, "A man's greatest pleasure in intimacy won't come when he experiences orgasm, but when he knows he's taken his bride to her ultimate sexual pleasure." For women, that may or may not include orgasm, it may be an emotional connection made while a husband pleasures his wife.[4] To do that, men need to stay in the game longer than the time it takes to pop a bag of microwave popcorn. Unfortunately our culture doesn't train men for sexual endurance or healthy conversations about sex. Since we were kids, we've associated sex with shame; we've let short-term pleasure steal from long-term satisfaction; and we've chased after bubbles more than cherished our brides.

Searching for Fig Leaves

I was nine years old when I saw my first copy of *Playboy*. I was ten when I saw my first porno movie. Neither was the fault of my parents. The first happened when the girl I was "going with" showed me a "secret" box under her dad's bed filled with women missing key pieces of clothing. The second happened at a birthday party where a mom thought it would be funny to watch a bunch of fourth graders blush. So she put on a movie where a woman kept taking off her clothes and jumping into bed with men. Though I hadn't instigated either incident, I still felt bad about what happened. Like a lot of boys, I learned to feel ashamed about sex before I even understood what it was or what God intended for it to be. I learned to hide my thoughts. I was thirteen when I had my first wet dream, and I soon discovered that I could cause my own version of a "wet dream" when I was awake. I had no idea it was called masturbation, I just knew it felt good. Let's be honest. It's fun, it's addictive, and when we're lonely, it provides a release. But let's also be honest about something else: sexual pleasure outside of marriage and shame are inextricably intertwined. Even though no one told me that pornography or habitual masturbation were wrong, I always did both in secret. Whether we follow God or not, we instinctively know that there is something unique about sexual sin. To the highly sensual people in Corinth, Paul writes, "Flee from sexual immorality. Every other sin a person commits is outside the body, but the sexually immoral person sins against his own body" (1 Corinthians 6:18). Sexual experience outside of marriage creates shame that drives us to secrecy. That's why we jump off the computer when someone comes into the room, or we erase our Internet history, or we watch adult movies alone, or we hide our magazines in a "secret box." Unfortunately, we also carry that shame into our marriage relationship, where it corrupts the oneness that God intended between husbands and wives. Ever since Adam, we have felt shame, and we have searched for fig leaves.

Two groups in our society are afraid to talk about sex: parents and the church. Because of that, many couples in our society are also afraid to talk about sex—even though it's a central part of the marriage relationship. When we experience confusion and feelings of shame, we instinctively hide. And when our expectations go unmet—expectations created by a culture that isn't afraid to talk about sex, but that doesn't talk about it from a godly perspective—we tend to clam up rather than open up.

Claw-Foot Tubs and Cars

In the absence of teaching about sex from our parents and the church, we look elsewhere for information. We engage our curiosity, develop our desires, and build our expectations based on what we see in movies, magazines, and on the Internet. It's there we train our minds to think sex is about techniques and toned bodies. Movie stars have no flaws. They make love effortlessly to sensual background music in the most awkward places, like claw-foot tubs, in the backseat of cars, and on office desks. When you're six-foot-two, cars and tubs don't work, and desks don't have pillows. In the movies, they make love in the morning without brushing their teeth. The kids never run in on them or knock on the door as the freight train is moving toward the station. The couple always experiences mutual and multiple orgasms. It's easy to believe that if you just looked a certain way and did certain things, your sexual experience would skyrocket. Those hopes and expectations seep into the marriage bedroom. Wives feel as if they don't measure up unless they look a certain way or perform certain acts. Husbands feel frustrated because they want to try something different, or they don't have the supposed stamina of a porn star. Rather than talk about their concerns, the couple clams up and oneness remains elusive. The cycle continues until the bedroom fires simmer to nothing more than two matchsticks that light up periodically for a moment and then flame out. Eventually, the husband decides it's just not worth the energy. He decides to take matters in his own hands—literally. He settles for self-gratification.

Short-Circuiting a Man's Brain

To keep the home fires burning long into the twilight of your marriage, a man must nourish his wife's self-worth by mirroring her beauty, and he must refuse to chase after lust. If a man refuses to mirror his wife's beauty, she will not feel desired. Her bedroom experience will move from joy to duty. If a man's eyes continue to dart to everyone but his wife, he will shatter the mirror God designed to reflect beauty back to her. And if a man pursues pornography and habitual masturbation, he will discover that short-term lust steals from long-term satisfaction.

Suppose I offered you a million dollars. Number one, I'd be your new best friend. But suppose right after I handed you the money, someone else came up to you and offered to trade you your million for a thousand dollars. Would you trade? It's not a trick question. Of course not. Yet every day, men leave their homes with a million dollars and trade it for a thousand. They trade it when they click the link to a pornographic website. They trade it when they allow their eyes to look at every woman who walks by. They trade it when they pore through soft porn magazines and watch adult movies. We quickly exchange the promise of long-term satisfaction for the fleeting illusions of lust.

According to behavioral scientist Dr. William Struthers, a steady diet of pornography and masturbation will literally short-circuit God's design for sexual pleasure and intimacy in a man. In his book *Wired for Intimacy: How Pornography Hijacks the Male Brain*, Struthers paints the picture of an old-fashioned water pump he visited on a farm when he was a kid:

> It was situated in the center of a cement slab and would drip ferociously, long after you stopped pumping. Over the years the leftover dripping water had cut a trough from under the spigot to the edge of the slab. The trough was nearly two inches deep, and any standing water on the slab would be channeled into it, cutting it deeper.
>
> So it is with pornography in a man's brain. Because of the way that the male brain is wired, it is prone to pick up on sexually relevant cues. These cues trigger arousal and a series of neurological, hormonal and neurochemical events are set into motion. Memories about how to respond to these cues are set off and the psychological, emotional and behavioral response begins. As the pattern of arousal and response continues, it deepens the neurological pathway, making a trough.
>
> This neural system trough, along with neurotransmitters and hormones, are the underlying physical realities of a man's sexual experience. Each time that an unhealthy sexual pattern is repeated, a neurological, emotional and spiritual erosion carves out a channel that will eventually develop into a canyon from which there is no escape.[5]

In other words, when a man settles for short-term gain with masturbation, he short-circuits long-term sexual satisfaction with his wife. The enemy wants to steal, kill, and destroy (John 10:10) your joy in marriage. With instant and seemingly anonymous access to pornography, he's taking men out one mouse click at a time.

Fortunately, Dr. Struthers offers hope: "But if this corrupted pathway can be avoided, a new pathway can be formed. We can establish a healthy sexual pattern where the flow is redirected toward holiness rather than corrupted intimacy. . . . By deepening the 'holiness' pathways, we are freed from deciding to do what is right and good as they become part of our embodied nature."[6] God has wired you for long-term sexual satisfaction with your bride. But when we crave lust more than we cherish our wives, we short-circuit the wiring.

Chasing Bubbles

For some reason, when I got married, I thought the sex shop would be open 24/7. I didn't realize my wife would be keeping banker's hours. There were monthly bank holidays, and the branch wasn't always open for business when I thought it should be.

I also assumed that my lust switch would turn off when I walked down the aisle; that when I said, "I do," some mysterious chemical would be released into my brain to inhibit my eyes from looking at other beautiful women. If there is such a chemical, it dissipates after about forty-eight hours. For me, it ran out during our honeymoon in St. Thomas.

I think in some ways lust after marriage can be worse than before. Once you've seen your wife naked, it's easier to compare her body to all the images that flood our minds on a daily basis. And if we've bought into the cultural view of sex as toned bodies and techniques, it's easy to lust after fantasies instead of cherishing reality.

Echo was my Jack Russell terrier and the best dog on the planet. If you know anything about JRTs, you know they are big dogs trapped in small bodies, and they make the Energizer Bunny look like a couch potato. Finding ways to burn through Echo's energy took creativity. One day, I was out blowing soap bubbles with my kids, and I noticed Echo jumping after every bubble. He couldn't stand for any of them to touch the ground.

He jumped up and down like a jack-in-the-box stuck on "Pop Goes the Weasel," chomping down on the bubbles. Up and down, up and down, up and down. *Chomp! Chomp! Chomp!* I had found a great way to exercise my dog by just blowing air.

As I launched more bubbles his way, I thought, *He thinks each shiny bubble has substance. Man, it stinks to be him!* After a few minutes, Echo had expended nuclear stores of energy on shiny bubbles filled with nothing.

Every day, shiny bubbles pass by my eyes. When I travel and speak, I don't wear a clerical collar, so no one knows I'm a pastor. When I walk into the convenience store, I know where the *Maxim* magazines are, and a bubble goes by my eye. When I get to the hotel, I know that certain channels are available on the TV. Another shiny bubble. As I'm perusing videos on YouTube, links to other sites pop up. More shiny bubbles. The enemy sits back and wonders, *Will he bite? Will he bite? Just one glance.* Meanwhile, the Holy Spirit speaks to my conscience, *Don't let a quick glance steal the lasting joy I have for you.* But am I listening?

If you've ever chased soap bubbles and had one land on your tongue, you know that a lot of energy can go into something that is very unsatisfying. Every time Echo bit on a bubble, all he received was a bad taste in his mouth. But his compulsive little mind wouldn't let him stop.

No one wakes up one day and says, "Today, I'll get addicted to pornography," or, "Today, I'll cheat on my wife." Instead, men let short-term pleasure steal from long-term satisfaction one drip at a time, one shiny bubble at a time.

No man can fight this battle alone. Whenever I travel, I have a few "and" guys who call and ask me one question, "Brian, are you chasing any bubbles today?" Just the anticipation of that question helps me let the shiny orbs float by.

When you've associated shame with sex you will have far more expectations than conversations about sex. When you've trained your brain for short-term pleasure rather than long-term gain, you'll spend your life chasing empty bubbles instead of chasing and cherishing your bride.

GAME FILM

In Scripture, you'll find exposés of those who indulged in short-term desires (Judah in Genesis 38; David in 2 Samuel 11; and Solomon in Ecclesiastes 2:1–11) and those who abstained from what they craved in favor of a better, more enduring prize. Three principles help us avoid the corrupted pathways and create new ones.

The Job Principle: Bounce the eyes. Though Steve Arterburn popularized this principle in his great book *Every Man's Battle*, he snatched the tip from one of the oldest books in the Bible. Job, in defending his sanctified record to his three foolish advisors, says, "I have made a covenant with my eyes; how then could I gaze at a virgin?" (Job 31:1). The longer we keep the window shades open on our eyes, the easier it is to cut a pathway away from long-term sexual satisfaction.

The Joseph Principle: Don't think, flee. When Paul wrote to the Corinthians, "Flee from sexual immorality" (1 Corinthians 6:18), he could have rolled tape on Joseph from Genesis 39. Joseph, young and virile, fled from his sensual temptress, Mrs. Potiphar. Far from any friends or family, he probably could have gotten away with it. When an image pops up in e-mail, we surf by a certain movie, or that girl in the office makes advances, act first—flee!—and think later. The longer we process, the easier it is to justify our desires and cut a pathway away from long-term sexual satisfaction.

The Jesus Principle: Go to extreme measures. One of most perplexing passages in the Bible for me is when Jesus says, "You have heard that it was said, 'You shall not commit adultery.' But I say to you that everyone who looks at a woman with lustful intent has already committed adultery with her in his heart. If your right eye causes you to sin, tear it out and throw it away. For it is better that you lose one of your members than that your whole body be thrown into hell. And if your right hand causes you to sin, cut it off and throw it away. For it is better that you lose one of your members than that your whole body go into hell" (Matthew 5:27–30).

I know Jesus doesn't think that plucking out an eye or cutting off a hand will stop my battle with lust. (The only people I know missing both an eye and a hand are pirates. And from what I hear, they aren't saints.) Jesus shocks his audience to prove a point. Long-term gain is worth the short-term pain. Be willing to sacrifice in order to preserve something more valuable. Abstaining from sexual desire hurts our bodies, for a moment. Are we willing to go to extreme measures to cherish our wives? The greater the temptation, the greater the sacrifice to avoid it. One man who was addicted to Internet pornography removed Internet access from his home computer. Another moved the computer into a room where the monitor was visible to anyone who walked into the room. Other men install Covenant Eyes software on their computers. Others cancel cable or satellite TV. Billy Graham was known to ask hotel managers to remove the TV from his room when he traveled, just so he wouldn't be tempted. I've talked to men who have had multiple affairs but who want to salvage their marriages. They go to recovery groups on a regular basis. They know that the power of addiction lies in secrecy, so they share often and openly. Such measures may sound drastic, but men who want to avoid the trough of sexual addiction need to carve new pathways. They are willing to pluck out the images feeding their eyes and cut off the hand feeding them pornography.

God Wrote a Book About Sex

When God designed sex, he knew about the gap. Yet God designed sex for our long-term mutual joy. Next time your desire for short-term pleasure tempts you to sacrifice long-term satisfaction, read Proverbs 5–7. Here's just a sample of Solomon's godly wisdom:

> Drink water from your own cistern [translation:
>   have sex only with your wife],
>   flowing water from your own well.
> Should your springs be scattered abroad,
>   streams of water in the streets? [See, I'm not
>   the only one who uses innuendo!]

> Let them be for yourself alone,
>> and not for strangers with you.
> Let your fountain be blessed,
>> and rejoice in the wife of your youth,
>> a lovely deer, a graceful doe.
> Let her breasts fill you at all times with delight;
>> be intoxicated always in her love.
>
> (Proverbs 5:15–19)

Did you hear that? God wants you to have great sex. Let me say it again: God wants you to have great sex! And it's for a lifetime. Not just until your bodies sag and your metabolism slows down. Not just until you have kids. Not just until once a month seems frequent. God designed sex to be enjoyed with one person for a lifetime.[7]

God designed our bodies. He invented sex. He knows exactly how it's best experienced. Throughout the Bible, God speaks a great deal about prayer, but he doesn't devote an entire book to the topic. He talks about finances (more than heaven and hell), but you won't find a book dedicated to the subject. He even gives wonderful wisdom on marriage, but not in a separate book. Yet, out of the sixty-six books of the Bible, he decided that one would be purely devoted to the topic of sex. In the ancient Near East, Jewish boys were not allowed to read it until they were at least thirteen.

Unfortunately, rather than taking our cues from the creator of sex, we take them from our culture. We buy the lie that great sex is simply an act of passion between two people, rather than an expression of love between two lifelong mates. So we listen to pillow talk from airbrushed hotties on *Cosmo* rather than the one who said in his sex manual, "Love is strong as death. . . . Its flashes are flashes of fire, the very flame of the LORD" (Song of Solomon 8:6). He started the flame; he can keep the home fires burning.

Cherish Your Bride

Have you ever been to one of those barbecue cook-offs where men in aprons mill about their massive smokers? The night before, these purveyors of pork roll into the staging area and set up their tents. Long before sunup they start burning their mesquite, apple, or hickory wood. Once they get the temperature just right, they throw on the king of meats for pulled pork: Boston butts. Throughout the day they massage the coals, spray down flare-ups, turn the meat, and monitor the temperature. After a day of smoking, the men in aprons finally pull off the meat. For a few minutes they let it cool. Gloved hands pull the pork into juicy clumps. The smokiness seeps into your nostrils. They stack the strands high on a bun crowned with homemade sauce and cole slaw (if you're from the south). A full day of cooking devoured in minutes.

Imagine someone pulling into a barbecue cook-off 20 minutes before judging. He sets up a table with a microwave. He pops his meat in the microwave and sets the timer for 15 minutes. Ding. He slathers on some sauce and throws it on a bun. Ready! Let's eat. Everyone knows the best barbecue is slow-cooked.

The same is true of our marriage. You can't microwave oneness. Throughout the day, a husband who loves like Jesus stokes the home fires with encouragement, he sprays down communication flare-ups quickly, he monitors, and helps adjust, the temperature of his bride. But I come from work, barely say two words to Jen, gobble down dinner, answer a few e-mails, rinse off the kids, throw them into bed, say the dishes can wait until morning, brush my teeth, and jump into bed. Ding! Let's eat! For some reason Jen isn't as hungry as I am. Sexual intimacy is best slow-cooked. For a wife to be ready, she needs a full day of preparation.

If things grow chilly in the bedroom, chances are you're not slow-cooking the relationship in other rooms of the house. Your kitchen is warmed by microwaved conversations rather than meaningful communication. Your living room is heated more by the television than companionship.

Texting Turn-Ons

I was presenting a session on sexual intimacy at a conference one weekend. Instead of me teaching about how women respond differently than men do in sexual intimacy, I decided to let the women educate us. So I asked a couple hundred ladies the question, "What turns you on sexually?" I had them text me the answers and I read them to the guys. While some texts heated up the phone with sensuality (e.g., *sucking on my toes*, *wine helps*, and *when he dances naked*), by and large the majority of them had nothing to do with sexual techniques or their husbands' toned bodies (good thing for us). Here's a sampling:

→ Watching him take care of the kids
→ Being talked to softly and sweetly and told I'm beautiful during soft kisses
→ Nothing turns me on more than a man coming home from work.
→ Rubbing my back while I do the dishes
→ Teaching our daughter how to serve a volleyball or throwing the football with our son without me asking him to
→ My husband being the spiritual leader of the home
→ Nothing turns me on like a man who can cook a great meal and is interested in what turns me on.
→ Flirting followed by a clean house and candles
→ My man putting our kids to bed while I unwind
→ Gives me a great massage or just holds me
→ A loving back rub without immediate sexual advances
→ When my husband spends time with me without the expectation of sex
→ Conversation and hugs
→ When my husband prays with and for me
→ A man in a suit who looks sharp, smells great, and is giving his ENTIRE attention to me on a hot date that he planned
→ When my husband is into me fully. His mind and heart are with me only not sports, job, himself. When he is romantic I melt and the rest falls into place.
→ Nothing turns me on more than feeling understood and valued for me, not what I do.

→ My husband flirting with me throughout the day
→ Doing a Bible study
→ A confident and content man is very attractive. Push-ups don't hurt.
→ Nothing turns me on more than my husband going grocery shopping with me and reaching over and rubbing my arms when he knows I'm cold in the frozen food aisles.
→ When my husband isn't afraid to hold me in public

When I think about the "Top 10 Sex Secrets of the Stars" headline in those grocery-story magazines, I don't think "Teaching our daughter how to serve a volleyball" or "Doing a Bible study" or "Holding me in the freezer aisle" makes the list. When I ponder those texts, I hear women who desire a "slow-cooked" relationship. They desire a man who stoked their fires all day rather than just the 15 minutes before he turns out the light. Have you ever asked your bride, "What turns you on sexually?" As I look at that list, most of it's not difficult, and it doesn't require time at the gym five days a week. As one lady remarked, "push-ups don't hurt," but they aren't essential. Let's stop chasing empty bubbles that never satisfy and start cherishing the "wife of our youth" God promises will satisfy.

A Real Man Nourishes and Cherishes His Bride

A husband who wants to love like Christ loves will nourish and cherish his wife. He will consistently cater to her crucial need for his love. He will engage when he'd rather shrink back. By now you should be able to make up your own list of what a real husband does. But here are a few to get you started:

A real husband . . .

→ Learns his wife's playbook for feeling loved
→ Mirrors his wife's beauty
→ Resolves conflict rather than avoids it

→ Doesn't just drive to church; he drives the home spiritually
→ Chases romance more than bubbles
→ "Slow-cooks" the relationship

I bet you've seen countless lists on how to be a better husband. It's one thing to know what to do, but quite another to execute it. Paul slaps the poster of Jesus on my wall and calls me up: "Be like Jesus!" Michael never helped me play like him, but Jesus promises to help me love like him.

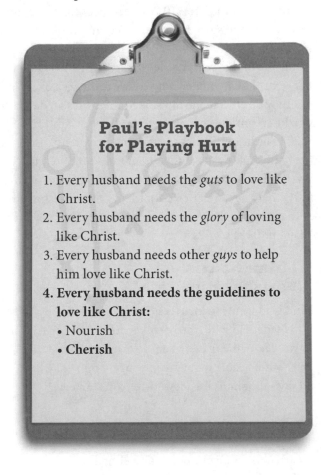

Paul's Playbook for Playing Hurt

1. Every husband needs the *guts* to love like Christ.
2. Every husband needs the *glory* of loving like Christ.
3. Every husband needs other *guys* to help him love like Christ.
4. **Every husband needs the guidelines to love like Christ:**
   - Nourish
   - **Cherish**

THE HOT SEAT

1. Of the three ways to cherish your wife, where is your greatest battle: conflict resolution, spiritual leadership, or sexual purity?

2. Have you established ground rules for conflict in your home? If not, name four or five you could share with your wife to start the conversation.

3. When was the last time you prayed with your wife other than before a meal? Find some time today to talk to your Father with her.

4. Are you chasing bubbles? What does that look like in your life? Who is one person you can confess your struggle to?

5. How are you at "slow-cooking" your relationship with your wife? What are two things you can do to help your wife feel cherished?

Chapter 8

The Power to Play Hurt

I COACH SOCCER FOR FIVE-YEAR-OLDS. No, it's not part of a work release program. My son loves the game. As a coach, I've discovered the most important part of the game happens before the first kick. I gather the Mighty Bees at midfield, look them all in the eye and ask, "What do we do, Bees?"

"Sting!" they all shout.

"Okay, Bees, which way are we going?"

Invariably, half the team points one way while the other half points the other. After pointing them all in the right direction and repeating myself about fifteen times, I'm pretty sure it's cemented in their brains. Even then, however, it has to stick in the heat of battle.

Once the game begins, I'm allowed to roam the field directing my Bees. I remember one particular kid who started dribbling the ball for the first time in a game. He shot up the field, passed midfield, and had an open lane to the opponent's goal. Parents cheered, I coaxed—and then time slowed down. He inexplicably turned around and started dribbling toward our own goal.

I tried my best not to morph into Bobby Knight, but I encouraged him loudly, "TURN AROUND! TURN AROUND!" He might as well have been David Beckham slicing through our team. He aimed at the corner. GOAL! He jumped up and down, turned around with arms raised above his head, and looked at his parents. They tried to hide under the bleachers.

It's one thing to know what to do, it's quite another to execute under game conditions. It's okay to head in the wrong direction if you're a five-year-old soccer player; it's quite another thing if you're five years, twelve years, twenty years into your marriage and you veer off course. Driving back from Atlanta with Jen, I knew where the right goal was. I could hear the Coach yelling in my ear, "Brian, turn around, look at your wife. Talk to her." I ignored him.

When we arrived home, I heard him say, "Don't let the sun go down on your anger." Instead, I charged down the field determined to go in the exact opposite direction and turn out the light.

My problem in marriage is not that I don't know what to do. I simply don't do it when the game is on the line. Even if ignorance were my problem, I can find great wisdom in the Bible. Every bookstore has wheelbarrows full of husband books. I can fill up my in-box with daily devotionals for men. I can load up my iPhone with countless podcasts on marriage. Men in our era have more solid guidance than any time in history. So why do we keep kicking the ball in the wrong direction?

→ You know you need to break the silence of an argument or keep silent during an argument, but you bury your feelings or explode in anger.

→ You know you shouldn't look at pornography and habitually masturbate, but you chase after bubbles.

→ You know you should learn your wife's primary love language, but you protest, *"No comprendo."*

→ You know you need to lead spiritually, but you rarely crack open a Bible or pray with your wife outside of mealtimes.

So, if it's not ignorance, maybe it's simply willpower. Maybe we just have a bunch of lazy husbands. I'd agree that passivity has affected men ever since Adam stood by while Eve went apple picking. But like great athletes, men who play hurt will ignore their feelings and gut it out. One reason that athletes can play through pain is simply because they can look at the clock. They know there's a time limit. "If I can just make it through this at bat, or this quarter, or this round, then I can rest."

It's easier to push through pain when we know it's almost over. But in marriage, there's no game clock. The horn sounds only when one player quits the game. Willpower works in games because anyone can override their feelings for short bursts of time. The wounds men face throughout marriage and life cannot be overcome by sheer guts alone; it requires help from our heavenly Father.

Connecting with the Father

It might be easy to read the previous chapter and think, "All I needed was a few fundamentals. Now I can finally be the husband I'm supposed to be. Whenever I'm wounded, I'll just gut through the pain like Michael Jordan did in Game 5 against the Utah Jazz. I'll nourish my wife's heart and cherish her, even when I don't feel like it."

But when Jesus set out on his mission to die for his bride, he never said, "I got this. I can handle it. I saw this at a conference once. Now that I have a few techniques, I'm all set."

Instead—130+ times in the book of John alone—Jesus talks about his dependence on his Father with statements like these:

The Father loves the Son and has given all things into his hand. (3:35)

For the Father loves the Son and shows him all that he himself is doing. And greater works than these will he show him, so that you may marvel. (5:20)

I have come in my Father's name. (5:43)

I live because of the Father. (6:57)

I and the Father are one. (10:30)

Before Jesus set out on his mission to die for his bride, he heard his Father say, "You are my beloved Son; with you I am well pleased" (Mark 1:11). When was the last time you believed God felt that way about you?

1. How would you describe your relationship with God in one word or phrase? Write it in the margin.
2. What does God think of you? Write it in the margin.

For most men, the *real* answer is different than the *right* answer. If you've been in the church for any length of time, you know "right" answers to the above questions: "Like a father and son" and "He loves me." But the *real* answers are probably more like these:

1. How would you describe your relationship with God in one word or phrase?
   "Distant."
   "Impersonal."
   "Untouchable."

2. What does God think of you?
   "I'm never good enough."
   "He's waiting for me to fail."

The right answers come from the head, but the real answers come from the heart. Men *know* that God is their Father and he loves them, but they've never really had a strong relationship with their earthly father so they're not sure what that *feels* like. I remember spending time with a life coach (aka psychotherapist, but no one likes to use that term) in Colorado. After two days of reviewing my rather uneventful, suburban past, I remember saying, "If all my struggles come down to the fact that I don't really believe God loves me and I've got issues with my dad, I'll be real upset with how much you're getting paid for this."

He crossed his legs, leaned back in his leather office chair, and said, "Yep, that's about it." He paused and then added, "I meet with very successful leaders from all over the country, and whether they are in the business world or the ministry world, most men are wounded because they don't inherently feel the love of God and they've got some lingering pain from their dad."

I walked down the aisle of my church to accept Jesus when I was nine years old. I decided to go into vocational ministry about the same time I got my driver's license. I went to a Bible college and then to seminary. Before I knew I liked girls, I knew the theological truth that God loved me, but it wasn't getting through to my heart. Turns out I had some clogged arteries (figuratively speaking).

Clogged Arteries

Clogged arteries don't just appear in middle age. They result from a buildup of a sticky substance called plaque that begins to develop on the inner arterial walls during childhood or the teenage years. But I've never heard someone ask a college kid, "Hey, how's your arterial plaque?" They have the energy of a hummingbird and their metabolism processes two Big Macs like a paper shredder through tissue paper. It's not until later, when our bodies react in ways we never expected—we feel shortness of breath on our morning run or tightness in our chest for no reason—that we think, *Huh, something might be wrong with my heart.* We then have a choice: Ignore it or get help.

Most of us don't recognize our heart wounds until we react in ways we never expected. We can't seem to get over self-doubt. We realize we crave constant approval from our bosses, our friends, our kids, and our wives. We promised ourselves we'd never get as angry as our parents, but then we got married. We've lost that loving feeling. We know we should love God, but we just don't. Chances are, the arterial plaque from earlier wounds, whether from Dad or someone else, is finally cutting off our connection to our wives or our heavenly Father. We don't know how to deal with the real heart matters in life:

handling emotional conflict, talking about sexual frustration, leading spiritually at home. We get shortness of breath, a tight feeling in our chest, and we have the choice: either ignore it or cry out for help. In conflict, we ignore the problem by attacking the other person with verbal hand grenades or bitter land mines. We ignore sexual frustration by running to temporary lusts rather than talking about and working toward long-term sexual satisfaction. We ignore spiritual leadership by going to church rather than walking with God. When the pain gets bad enough, we ignore it by medicating ourselves with hobbies and addictions.

Ignore these issues long enough and we're bound to suffer a spiritual heart attack. Our hearts stop beating for our wives or for God. It's no surprise that most guys get far more excited going to a basketball game than going to church. We can feel the glory on the court, but can't connect with the glory of the Father in the pew. We read the Bible, pray, and serve because we know it's something we ought to do, but we rarely feel God's pleasure in it. We start defining oneness in marriage as agreeing on the same TV show, equal time out with friends, and nights that pass without conflict. Denying pain because we're disconnected from the Father isn't playing hurt, it's playing stupid.

Do you know the name Sam Bowie? Unless you're nearing middle age and love basketball trivia, I'm guessing you've never heard of him. He'll forever be known as the guy picked before Michael Jordan in the 1984 NBA draft. The Portland Trailblazers still get called out for that one. However, to be fair to them, they didn't need another guard as much as they needed help on the front line. No one could predict that Sam Bowie would be so injury prone and Jordan so championship prone. There's a reason why we have a category called draft day busts. High expectations rarely match performance. But what if in 1984 someone gave Portland a sports magazine from 2000 headlining Jordan as the basketball player of the century? What if someone gave them a VHS tape[1] with all his future highlights? On draft day they'd have been fools not to call out his name.

We know God's highlights. Our Bible headlines him as all-powerful. We'd be a fool not to call out his name. But how many of us really do? Our best prayer times are in front of our dinner plates. We may give God lip service, but I'd imagine most of us feel as if we have clogged arteries in our relationship with him; so we just stop calling. How do we unclog the blockage? We need to admit we need help and get a bypass.

Admit You Need Help

When a doctor asks you, "What seems to be the problem?" you list off your symptoms: I can't walk up a flight of stairs without needing an oxygen tank; I eat a taco and get sharp pangs in my chest. So how come when another guy asks you what's wrong with your marriage, you say, "Nothing. We're fine. Maybe not perfect, but better than most"?

We're afraid to expose our pain.

That's why I love the Psalms. It's a pain blog. You can read one a day and get through the whole book twice in a year. These warrior poets wielded a pen as well as a sword. They were man enough to admit they had more than a flesh wound:

I am weary with my moaning; every night I flood my bed with tears. (6:6)

My God, my God, why have you forsaken me? Why are you so far from saving me, from the words of my groaning? (22:1)

O LORD my God, I cried to you for help, and you have healed me. (30:2)

God's not afraid of our pain. In fact, until we open up our wounds, he can't heal us. I'm not sure where you stand in your relationship with God, but he has a vested interest in your success. As we discussed in chapter 2, your marriage is anything but ordinary; it's a visual symbol of an eternal reality. People from our kids, to our neighbors, to our coworkers are watching your marriage as a movie of God's glory. It offers a glimpse of the gospel to a world that largely ignores God. Fortunately, he doesn't require an Oscar-worthy performance. He's not a distant director barking orders from a chair: "Can't you get that line right?! You idiot! Sacrifice like you mean it! When are we going to get someone in here who can actually play the role of husband?"

Directors yell, "Action!" and expect the actors to perform. *How was that take, God? Watch this. I'll get it right this time. One more chance, God. Aren't you impressed?* That's one reason why God feels so distant in our lives. We know he loves us theoretically, but it's hard to experience love from someone in a director's chair.

God never intended to sit on the sidelines. He's got too much at stake in our marriages for you or I to go it alone. The adversary we face can't be dealt with in our own strength. We're too wounded. We're too selfish. And we're not strong enough.

In most twelve-step programs, the recovering addicts recite step 1 on a regular basis: "We admitted we were powerless over our addiction—that our lives had become unmanageable." That doesn't mean you're a wimp. It just means you're strong enough to admit you're not strong enough.

Not only do we need to admit that our wounds hurt, but we must admit we have wounded our heavenly Father. Every time I say, do, or think something contrary to God's character, I hurt him. I'm glad he doesn't issue tickets with each infraction.

As I write this, I'm in a coffee shop. A lady in a tight black dress walks by. My heavenly father thinks, *That's one of my daughters. I wonder what Brian is thinking about her. Oh . . .*

"AHHH!" I shout with Paul, "Wretched man that I am! Who will deliver me from this body of death?" (Romans 7:24). I must admit to God that I'm just like my dad, who was just like his dad, who was just like his dad, all the way back to Adam. You may not be exactly like your alcoholic father, but you get angry. You may not be like your philandering dad, but you love that Victoria's Secret catalog. You may not be like your absent father, but you do whatever it takes to get noticed by others. The Bible calls this arterial plaque *sin*. It's a self-inflicted buildup. We all have it and will die because of it (Romans 6:23). The only question is what you will do with that prognosis. Some believe that because they go to church, live a better life than most people they know, pay their taxes on time, brake for animals, and raise relatively well-adjusted kids, they will be fine. That's like imagining healthy living alone can cure a clogged artery.

God says not only do we need to be healed from our wounds, but we need to be released from our reliance on healthy living. Our good behavior doesn't heal our relationship with him. Imagine telling a doctor who has just informed you that you need bypass surgery or you will die, "It's okay, I'll just eat better and exercise."

"No, you don't get it; it won't be enough."

"I'll take my chances."

Your healthy living might mask the symptoms for a while, but eventually the clog will claim your life. The Bible says, "No one seeks for God. All have turned aside; together they have become worthless; no one does good, not even one" (Romans 3:11–12). Paul said to the church in Galatia, "I do not nullify the grace of God, for if righteousness were through the law, then Christ died for no purpose" (Galatians 2:21). Righteousness (or justification) simply means "being right with God." He defines connection to the Father not through "works of the law" (Romans 3:20) or moral health. In other words, you can take Mother Teresa's playbook and run all the right plays, but it won't be enough to unclog your blocked artery with God. You need a bypass.

Bypass Surgery

I've never read a book called *Heart Surgery for Dummies* or *Do It Yourself: Bypass Surgery*. "You can do it. We can help!" For most of my life, I've heard that connecting with God requires far more effort on my part than on his. Pray more. Read more. Study more. Do more. Be more. My effort equals his pleasure.

I've lived under the assumption that when I'm working hard for God, he's noticing my effort. It's like we've got a contract. I do well by him and maybe he'll do well by me. Eventually, things don't go well and I assume I haven't lived up to expectations; or worse, that somehow he's overlooked my good behavior.

Not surprisingly, I translated the same attitude into my marriage. When things don't go well with Jen, I assume it's because I'm not living up to my side of the bargain or God is not rewarding me for my good behavior.

But here's the thing: God calls us to a relationship, not to a contract.

God never promised to fix your marriage. He never promised to change your wife's heart or condition. He simply asked you to love his daughter like his Son loved us. That radical love is impossible without his help. Jesus couldn't do it alone; what makes me think I can?

When I was growing up, I heard many gospel presentations. The first one I remember was when I was nine years old. The college drama team put on a very convincing show about the torments of hell. They clearly communicated how even one sin punches a one-way ticket to the eternal fiery furnace. At nine, my rap sheet included cussing and stealing change from my parents' change jar. But I didn't want to be on that train. When the leader asked if anyone wanted to trust Christ, I shot up my hand.

Now, it's true that our sin separates us from God. It's true that punishment is forever. But the good news is not about our running away from hell; it's about God running toward us. It's about recognizing we are all prodigal sons who desperately need the extravagant love of the Father. The gospel is far more about what he has done for us than what we do for him.

We understand the gospel when we realize that we need to be rescued from our badness *and* our goodness. That, because of Jesus' sacrifice, our sin doesn't hurt our standing with the Father and our goodness doesn't get his attention. In other words, when we turn away from sin and toward Jesus, he reconnects us with the Father. God doesn't yell at us when we blow it, and he doesn't grade us for our good performance. The only thing that gets his attention is when we turn from trying to please him (self-righteousness) or ourselves (selfish desires) and follow his Son.

I have a friend who asks his son, "Jack, who are you?" He

taught his son to respond, "I'm Daddy's boy." The dad asks, "Jack, when does that change?" The son replies, "Never."

Paul prays in the book of Ephesians:

> For this reason I bow my knees before the Father . . . that according to the riches of his glory he may grant you to be strengthened with power through his Spirit in your inner being, so that Christ may dwell in your hearts through faith—that you, being rooted and grounded in love, may have strength to comprehend with all the saints what is the breadth and length and height and depth, and to know the love of Christ that surpasses knowledge, that you may be filled with all the fullness of God. (3:14–19)

Paul prays diligently for God to help the Ephesians "comprehend" the incredible love of God. This isn't Oprah-style self-help. It's being gripped with how great the affections of God are for his children. Paul uses similar language in Romans 8:38–39, when he says that cosmic crusaders or death itself can't separate us from the love of God. But I can't even grasp the concept of God's love for me without God's help. That's why Paul prays. That's why Jesus tells the religious leader, Nicodemus, that he must be "born again" (John 3:7). It means to be born from above. I'm sure Nicodemus wanted a study guide on how he could make that happen. Jesus talked about a surgeon coming to do a bypass on Nicodemus's heart. Nicodemus needed to believe that only God can deal with the arterial plaque in his heart. Jesus called the surgeon, the Holy Spirit, and like a wind, he comes when he's ready.

Have you received a bypass from God? Jesus preached one message to humanity, "Repent . . ." (Matthew 4:17). Repent is a fancy word that means to do a 180. He called people to turn from their path and follow his path. To be "born again" we must come to a place where we stop trying to please God through our self-righteous behavior or to please ourselves through selfish desires. If you sense a stirring in your heart, then the Spirit is blowing. Cry out to God. He will come to your rescue (Romans 10:9–11, 13).

Paul says that all sons of God are led by this Spirit (Romans 8:14). In fact, we can't even call God "Daddy" without the Spirit's help (Romans 8:15). Our connection with the Father depends on his Spirit. What does this have to do with marriage? Without the Spirit helping me connect with the Father, I won't have the power to be like Jesus.

It Must Be the Shoes

In 1985, Nike unleashed the first Air Jordan basketball shoes. They were black streaked with red. Michael Jordan was fined $5,000 every time he wore the shoes in a game because they violated the league's uniform policy. That only heightened my desire to own a pair. Those sneaks cost about $65 at the time. That equated to mowing about three yards. I mowed the grass and I bought the shoes. I remember lacing them up like Mike did in the commercials. I think they put about three centimeters on my vertical the first time I went up for a layup. If Nike could have sold a shoe that guaranteed I could jump as high and play as well as Mike, I would have mowed three hundred yards to buy them. Sadly, they never made that shoe; but I never stopped trying to be like Mike.

Two thousand years ago, God came out with a sacrifice streaked with red. It cost him everything. He said that if you put on his Son, you'd love like he does. You'd have the power to resist a much stronger enemy, to nourish and cherish a bride like he would, and to love without expecting anything in return. God won't sell you that sacrifice, but he will give it to you. It's available to any husband who desires it; but sadly, many men won't apply it to their lives.

In basketball, I practiced and practiced to be like Mike, but I just didn't have the physical ability to get to his level. In marriage, however, if we have believed in the gospel, God grants us the supernatural ability to love like Jesus. But we don't just put on the shoes. Paul says to the Galatians, "But I say, walk by the Spirit" (Galatians 5:16).

Plugged Into the Spirit

How would you describe your relationship with the Holy Spirit in one word or phrase?

How does he empower your marriage?

Once again, I bet the *real* answer will be different from the *right* answer. I wonder if the word that came to mind was *convicter.* Jesus said that when the Holy Spirit came, he would "convict the world concerning sin and righteousness and judgment" (John 16:8).

The Holy Spirit is the one who lets us know when we shouldn't yell at our wives, or click that website, or kick the dog. He's like a "check engine" light that blinks when something's wrong with our spiritual engine. Though the Spirit lets us know when we stray from God's character, Jesus had an even better name for him: *Helper* (John 14:16, 26). Jesus spoke about how the Spirit helps us move far more than he reveals where we mess up.

So how does he help us move in our marriages?

When I think about the areas where I often struggle in my marriage—resolving conflict, leading spiritually, and dealing with romance/sexual issues—I may seek help from books and conferences, but I rarely think about the Spirit desiring to help me. Nothing wrong with wisdom, tips, and techniques, but ultimately I need power I don't naturally possess to love like Jesus.

GAME FILM

Listen to one of the craziest verses in the Bible. In the upper room, where Jesus ate a last meal with his friends the night before his death, he made a comment that I'm not sure sank in with his audience: "Truly, truly, I say to you, whoever believes in me will also do the works that I do; and greater works than these he will do" (John 14:12).

Did you catch that? Whoever believes in Jesus will do greater works than he did. Then he tells them that the Holy Spirit will come to be their Helper to do these greater works. In Acts 1:8, Jesus speaks again about the Spirit giving the disciples power.

We think of the Spirit as giving us nice spiritual gifts, like administration, or leadership, or teaching. We think of the Spirit as convicting us when we mess up. But do we think of the Spirit as a powerful being who wants to do "even greater things than Jesus did" through us? What could be greater than healing the blind, raising the dead to life, and making a buffet out of a boxed lunch?

Jesus responds with, "Greater love has no one than this, that someone lay down his life for his friends" (John 15:13). Jesus is a perfect God loving imperfect people unconditionally for a lifetime. The only thing greater than that would be if God's *imperfect* people loved other imperfect people unconditionally for a lifetime.

When Jesus was willing to die for us, we can say, "Well, he is God." When a husband pursues his wife after she cheated on him, again; when a husband stops the cycle of abuse; when a husband cherishes his bride who has a degenerative disease, for three decades, we say, "Wow, how did he do that?" Only one explanation, it must be the shoes.

Jesus talks about the Spirit in John 14:16–31 and John 16:4–15. In between those bookends, he tells his disciples that they will abide and treasure Christ (John 15:1–11); love sacrificially (15:12–17); endure gratefully (15:18–25); and share fearlessly (15:26–16:4). Before Jesus died on the cross, these disciples did none of these things well. Let's look at a few of the men who were there at Jesus' last supper:

→ Thomas was a fearful doubter.
→ Peter, the antithesis of Theodore Roosevelt, spoke loudly but carried a small stick. Later that night, he hit the snooze button on prayer. Eventually, he denied he even knew Jesus and ran from a servant girl who identified him as a disciple.
→ Matthew was hated by his countrymen as a tax collector.
→ Simon the Zealot polarized people who didn't agree with his political views.
→ John and James were fishermen who were known as uneducated and common men.

Before Jesus went to the cross, these men bickered and jockeyed for position. They lacked the resumes to build a huge organization. On that fateful night, we have a much more detailed record of their failures than their successes. But Jesus said greater things were in their future when the Helper would come.

After Jesus rose from the dead and ascended to heaven, his disciples were changed men. If you peruse the book of Acts, you will notice how this ragtag group of self-focused, comparison driven, weak-willed, cowardly men dramatically changed. You'll discover that these same disciples, in just fifty days, treasured Jesus more than their own lives, loved others so much they sold their own houses, endured jails with joy, and could not help but share the message of God's rescue mission for mankind.

What happened? They got the right shoes.

You may not feel as if you have the right tools to build a marriage. Right now, you may be more defined by your failures than by your successes in your marriage. You may be self-focused, too scared to speak up, or desire vindication for your wounds more than victory in your marriage. You're in good company.

We invite God the Father to the wedding day, but leave him at the altar during the marriage. He wants us to lace up and "walk in the Spirit."

"But Brian, you don't know my wife; she nags me like nails on a chalkboard."

"But Brian, my addictions and battle with self-worth are like thorns in my side."

"But Brian, I just don't think I can make it another day."

Ironically, the role model whom God asks us to follow knows a little something about nails and thorns. He's endured far more than we ever will. And he's ready to give us the same power. The gospel doesn't sink in—it's not about what we can do for God, but what God has already done and will do for us. He's got far more vested in your relationship with your bride than you do. And he's waiting for you to let him help. He's like Tom Cruise's character in *Jerry Maguire*: "Help me help you! Help me help you! Help me help you." He wants to help you do greater things in your marriage than you can imagine.

How? Paul challenges us to "be strong in the Lord and in the strength of his might" (Ephesians 6:10). God's not looking for willpower and good techniques. He wants men brave enough to depend on his strength more than their own.

Lean Forward

I have a friend who used to train as part of the Olympic ski team. He had a European coach who pushed these guys to the limit. Downhill racers typically run about fifty or sixty miles per hour. At one spot on the mountain, there was a sudden descent off of a turn. Most skiers would be caught off guard and instinctively lean back. In that split second, they made a choice that resulted in lost speed or falling backwards. The coach started positioning himself right before the dip so he could yell to the skiers: "LEAN FORWARD!" He gradually trained them to forget their instincts and lean forward.

When we lace up the shoes of the Spirit, Paul warns us, "The desires of the flesh are against the Spirit, and the desires of the Spirit are against the flesh, for these are opposed to each other" (Galatians 5:17). Every follower of Christ is a tortured soul. Our instincts tell us to pull back, to be passive, to take a temperature, to desire vindication, to clam up or cuss. Meanwhile, the Spirit is shouting, "LEAN FORWARD!"

Stick close to the Spirit and don't lose your momentum in marriage. Engage. Be a thermostat. Desire victory. Resolve conflict. Talk about your sexual frustration. Don't bite the bubble.

There's a second or two in my marriage when I make a decision to lean back or lean forward. I know what to do, but when I lean back I trust my instincts over God's Spirit. God doesn't just want us to know the goal; he wants to help us run the race to victory.

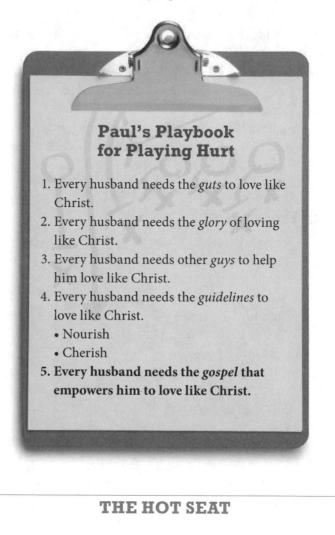

Paul's Playbook for Playing Hurt

1. Every husband needs the *guts* to love like Christ.
2. Every husband needs the *glory* of loving like Christ.
3. Every husband needs other *guys* to help him love like Christ.
4. Every husband needs the *guidelines* to love like Christ.
   - Nourish
   - Cherish
5. **Every husband needs the *gospel* that empowers him to love like Christ.**

THE HOT SEAT

1. Do you find that you know what to do, but just don't do it? Why is that?

2. Did you answer the two questions about the Father?

   a. Describe your relationship with God in one word or phrase.

   b. How do you think God feels about you?

3. Have you admitted you need God's help to overcome your wounds from the past? Have you admitted to him you need to be forgiven for the way you've wounded him?

4. Did you answer the two questions about the Holy Spirit?

   a. Describe your relationship with the Spirit in one word or phrase.

   b. How does he empower your marriage?

5. What's one way you can lean forward in your marriage this week?

Chapter 9

New Posters for Your Wall

As KIDS, THE REASON WE DECKED our walls with posters of star athletes was because we believed that maybe, just maybe, we could make that shot, hit that ball, or shoot that puck like our heroes. After all, they weren't superheroes from another planet. They grew up in some neighborhood just like we did. They got hurt just like we did. I mean, it wasn't likely . . . but it was possible.

It's important to have role models, someone to look up to. Since I've started down this road, I try to keep a few posters of men who model this radical way to love their wives. You won't find their numbered jersey at Sports Authority, but I consider them all-stars.

I'll tell you their stories just so you know it's possible to love your wife like Christ loves the church. These guys grew up in a neighborhood, just like we did. They aren't superheroes. They get hurt just like we do. They just keep playing hurt.

Mike

At two o'clock one morning, Victoria shook Mike awake.

"Mike, get up. Get dressed and go get in the car."

Mike rubbed the sleep out of his eyes, "What's wrong? Are the kids on fire?"

"Would you just listen to me? Get up. Get dressed. Hurry."

Mike reluctantly got out of bed, threw on some clothes, and got in the car.

As they pulled out of the driveway, Mike asked, "Victoria, what about the girls?"

She replied, "They're taken care of. Just enjoy the drive."

When they arrived at the airport, Victoria parked the car and popped the trunk. She pulled out two prepacked suitcases. When they got to the ticket counter, she produced two tickets to the Virgin Islands. It was Mike's fortieth birthday. For the past few *years*, Victoria had been secretly saving money from teaching aerobics. She had planned a week with everything Mike would love: eating at great restaurants, scuba diving, and totally renaming the Virgin Islands.

After they returned, they went to a party and some of their friends prompted them to tell their story. Afterward, some guy approached Victoria and asked her in a low voice, "You know, it's my fortieth birthday coming up. I was wondering if you'd put in a good word with my wife about what you did for Mike."

Victoria, who might be five-foot-two, looked up at the guy, pointed her finger at his sternum, and said through clenched teeth, "If you would love your wife half as much as Mike loves me, then I wouldn't have to say a thing."

Of course, the guy was stunned. "Okay," he said. "So is that a no?"

Mike's an all-star, not because he's perfect, but because for years he nourished his wife's heart without expecting anything in return. Mike's tough, but you can't love like that naturally. He leaned forward, down the mountain, and into the wind.

The Professor

I've heard about this story for years, but I finally found documentation of it a few days ago. In March 1990, the year I graduated from high school, Dr. Robertson McQuilkin "graduated" from being president of Columbia Bible College. His wife, Muriel, was suffering from advanced stages of Alzheimer's and he was resigning in order to be able to care for her. He presented a letter to the university that explained his thinking:

> Perhaps it would help you to understand if I shared with you what I shared at the time of the announcement of my resignation in chapel. The decision was made, in a way, forty-two years ago when I promised to care for Muriel "in sickness and in health . . . till death do us part." So, as I told the students and the faculty, as a man of my word, integrity has something to do with it. But so does fairness. She has cared for me fully and sacrificially all these years; if I cared for her for the next forty years, I would not be out of debt. Duty, however, can be grim and stoic. But there is more; I love Muriel. She is a delight to me—her happy spirit and tough resilience in the face of her continual distressing frustration. I do not have to care for her. *I get to!* It is a high honor to care for so wonderful a person.[1]

Dr. McQuilkin counted it a privilege to leave a profession that he knew so well, and where he was regarded highly, in order to care for his bride, who would slowly forget him. He's an all-star.

Greg

Ever argue on the way to church because you've been rushing to get everyone there on time? Check out my friend Greg's morning before church:

- → Wake up. Wake Lisa up.
- → Brush teeth. Brush Lisa's teeth.
- → Take a shower with Lisa. (It's just easier to wash her hair that way.)
- → Dry his own hair. Dry and style Lisa's hair.
- → Shave. (He does that solo.)
- → Pick out Lisa's clothes and then something for himself that matches.

↝ Make sure the four kids are dressed and ready for church.

↝ Fix breakfast for everyone.

↝ Load the kids. Load Lisa—which means lifting her from the bed to the wheelchair, and from the wheelchair to the car.

↝ Drive to church.

↝ Lift Lisa out of the car and into her wheelchair.

↝ After church, repeat the process in reverse: out of the wheelchair and into the car; out of the car at home and into the wheelchair; out of the wheelchair into the bed.

↝ Then it's time to get lunch ready for everyone.

Hopefully he didn't forget his Bible at church.

And that's just Sunday morning.

During the week, if you ask Greg to go out for lunch, he'll probably say no. He likes to spend it with Lisa at the house. Plus, it means one less trip back to the house during the day. He usually needs to go back four or five times to take care of any need she might have: calculating her food and feeding it through the tube; being a health-care nurse and dealing with medications, catheterizations, and all her feminine needs.

Here's the back story: Four years into their marriage, Greg and Lisa were in seminary preparing for ministry. They wanted to pastor somewhere in the Midwest, preferably in a farming community like the one Greg grew up in. Lisa worked at a bank as an executive assistant. One ordinary day, Lisa started seeing double and a little fuzzy. After a few days of these weird symptoms, they finally got her eyes checked out.

"From what we can tell, it's either a tumor, the onset of a potential aneurism, or multiple sclerosis)," the doctor said. *Can I pick D—none of the above?* thought both Greg and Lisa. A neurologist confirmed it was MS. Lisa received a few steroid shots, hoping the symptoms would subside. They did, but not because of the steroids.

For the next five years, Greg and Lisa had four kids. The pregnancies kept the MS at bay. Six months after their last son was born, on a trip to Israel (Greg's a licensed tour guide), Lisa felt paralysis on her left side, and then loss of bladder control. Soon, she had her own "rolling throne." One picture from that trip encapsulates the next *twenty-five* years of their marriage. While going through the old city of Jerusalem, with its countless steps and uneven levels, Greg and three others helped carry Lisa in her wheelchair up the Via Dolorosa, which means "Way of Suffering." Two thousand years ago, Jesus, having been whipped and scourged, toted a heavy beam up the same path. When Greg hears Jesus' call to his followers, "Take up your cross daily and follow me," I think he gets it.

After they returned from Israel, Lisa's doctor pulled Greg aside and confirmed what they had suspected. The MS was here to stay. She would probably lose use of her arms and legs, and her vision would probably get worse. The doctor looked at Greg and said, "This is the time most spouses pull out."

On their wedding day, Greg had stood before Lisa, a former gymnast and sprinter in high school, and promised to love her "for better or for worse," "for richer or for poorer," and "in sickness or in health." Now, just a few years later he was living the "for worse," "for poorer," and "in sickness" part. After a diagnosis of multiple sclerosis, 70 to 80 percent of spouses leave the marriage. At a seminar on the disease, Greg and Lisa sat at a table with ten other people. Of the ten, six were single women whose husbands had left them after they contracted the disease. Greg has heard all the excuses from spouses who want out:

"I know she wouldn't expect me to stick around."
"This wasn't what I signed up for."
"God wouldn't want me to go through something like this."

His response is, "Really? I'm glad Jesus didn't say the same things."

Jesus found joy in enduring the cross because he trusted God's plan more than his own feelings. Greg and Lisa accepted that their dreams for life didn't match God's plan; but they find joy despite their circumstances. Lisa's had plenty of ups and downs. A couple of years ago, she was given six months to live. But so far she's beaten the odds. She was recently wheeled down the aisle at her oldest son's wedding. The family still gathers around her bed for pizza night. They find humor in the mundane moments. Greg came home one night and one of Lisa's eyes had shut so it looked like she was winking at him. Greg said, "Are you trying to seduce me?" Lisa replied, "If it works!"

Certainly, it's never easy to care for someone with a debilitating disease, whether it's Alzheimer's, cancer, or MS. You almost expect it in the twilight of your marriage, but not at sunrise, not at midday. Greg was my boss at the seminary for more than a year. He loved laughter, lots of good food, and Lisa. When I went home at night, Jen and I would watch *Seinfeld* reruns and figure out where we wanted to go for dinner. When Greg left the school, he started his second and third shifts. He clocked in at home as a cook, housekeeper, nurse, tutor, nanny, husband, and dad.

Watching Greg and Lisa is like watching an instant classic of God's unconditional love. When Lisa apologizes for the loss of her arms and legs, Greg tells her, "I did not marry you for what you could do, but for who you are. Every one of us will be limited in what we can do, and it will be at that time we impact people based on who we are. The beautiful wrapping does not last long, but a good gift does."

Though I never want to play through the pain that Greg and Lisa have endured, I hope I have the courage if put in a similar situation. I imagine when God calls Greg and Lisa home, they'll both be running around the bases, fist pumping the whole way. I know Greg has already knocked the ball out of the park. He's an all-star.

Joel

When I was sixteen, I traveled with my dad to his boyhood farm in North Carolina. A hurricane had blown through and crumpled the old barn, and we were going to see what could be salvaged. Granddad had passed away when I was barely into kindergarten, but I still had a few memories. Underneath one of the beams of the fallen barn was the old tractor I remembered driving through the fields on Granddad's lap. My step-grandmother was still living on the farm, though most of the fields were fallow. We started pulling out rakes, garden tools, and anything of use. I noticed dad stacking a few jars filled with a clear yellow liquid.

"What's that?"

"Oh," Dad responded with a slight cough, "that's my dad's homemade brew."

"What's it taste like?"

"Gasoline." He didn't offer much else.

Some stories started surfacing in my mind from a few pieced-together conversations.

As I stared into the jars of original "mountain dew," I realized I never knew what it was like to have a father who secretly stashed an addiction. I didn't know what it was like to have a dad who screamed and cursed when he got drunk. I didn't have memories etched in my mind of his mom lying on the floor while dad yelled at her, "If you get up, I'll kill you." As I stacked the thirteen jars of moonshine, I realized that my dad had reversed the curse and had spared me from similar wounds. Though my dad's upbringing had been hard, he had decided that his scars wouldn't define his life. He had left the hardscrabble farm and had built a life where hurricanes wouldn't expose dark secrets.

Joel Goins didn't allow a broken connection with his dad to become a broken connection with his bride or his kids. He's an all-star. By the way, thanks, Dad.

Notes

Chapter 3: The Motivation to Play Hurt

1. Act 4, scene 3.
2. J. Strong, *Strong's Enhanced Lexicon* on Libronix, electronic ed. (Ontario: Woodside Bible Fellowship, 1996), number 3173.

Chapter 4: The Real Enemy

1. Mike High, personal conversation in 2001 as he discussed his research of strong families when he worked for FamilyLife.

Chapter 5: Allies Every Husband Needs

1. Bill and Caroyln Wellons authored a great workbook, *Getting Away to Get It Together*, that walks you through a "marriage physical." You clear out a weekend every six months or a year and walk through their questions. It's something you can revisit year after year.

Chapter 6: A Husband's Nutritional Guide

1. Excerpted from Tom Chiarella, "The 75 Skills Every Man Should Master," *Esquire*, May 5, 2008, http://www.esquire.com/features/essential-skills-0508#ixzz19PtkpGW8.
2. I'm indebted to Robert Lewis who first took me through the Men's Fraternity discipleship training program, which gave me a biblical definition of manhood. A real man rejects passivity, accepts responsibility, leads courageously, and expects God's greater reward. Find the study at www.mensfraternity.com.

3. Shaunti Feldhahn and Jeff Feldhahn, *For Men Only* (Sisters, OR: Multnomah, 2006), 27–28.

4. Ibid., 44.

5. Ibid., 33 (emphasis in the original).

6. Gary Chapman, *The Five Love Languages: How to Express Heartfelt Commitment to Your Mate* (Chicago: Northfield, 2004), 107.

7. Feldhahn and Feldhahn, *For Men Only*, 151–54. The entire chapter is a must-read.

8. Ibid., 155.

Chapter 7: Become a Thermostat, Not a Thermometer

1. Earl D. Radmacher, Ronald B. Allen, and H. Wayne House, eds., *The Nelson Study Bible: New King James Version* (Nashville: Thomas Nelson, 1997), 1933.

2. Here are a couple of tools I like to keep handy: *Marriage Forecasting: Changing the Climate of Your Relationship One Conversation at a Time* by Tim Muelhoff; and *Fight Fair: Winning at Conflict Without Losing at Love* by Tim and Joy Downs.

3. Whether you read the Alfred Kinsey reports on human sexuality or turn on Dr. Phil, you will find this gap between the average time it takes for men and women to achieve orgasm; http://www.drphil.com/articles/article/99 (accessed February 3, 2011).

4. According to Jeff and Shaunti Feldhahn, about 16 percent of women do not experience orgasm during sex with their husbands, *For Men Only*, 137. How excited would you be about sex if you never achieved orgasm?

5. William M. Struthers, *Wired for Intimacy: How Pornography Hijacks the Male Brain* (Downers Grove, IL: InterVarsity, 2009), 106.

6. Ibid., 106–7.

7. I recognize that many factors affect sexual enjoyment. Psychological, mental, physical, and health issues all have an impact on a couple's intimacy. Often an outside voice can help determine steps that may help. This is where a professional can offer great coaching tips as well as discuss medical options, if necessary. Because God invented sex for procreation and pleasure, we should not be ashamed to discuss it with our wives, or to get help when needed.

Chapter 8: The Power to Play Hurt

1. For those who didn't grow up in the '80s, a VHS tape was how we recorded shows before the advent of DVRs.

Chapter 9: New Posters for Your Wall

1. Robertson McQuilkin, *A Promise Kept: The Story of an Unforgettable Love* (Wheaton, IL: Tyndale, 1998), 22 (emphasis in the original).

About the Author

BRIAN GOINS AND HIS BRIDE of fifteen years, Jennifer, set up shop in Charlotte, North Carolina, with their three kids (Brantley, Palmer, and Gibson). He, along with a great team, serves as pastor at Renaissance Bible Church (renbible.org).

Brian and Jennifer also travel around the country speaking to couples at Weekend to Remember events for FamilyLife. He received his Masters of Theology degree from Dallas Theological Seminary and worked as creative director for Insight for Living before going into church ministry. Brian bleeds Tarheel blue, remembers when he played basketball, wishes he was a carpenter, and wants to figure out how to live in Montana six months out of the year.

Tell Brian your favorite "playing hurt"
athletic story at playinghurt.org.